COSTA RICA RETIREMENT: 3RD EDITION LIVING ON $400 PER MONTH

BY
PETER MICHAELS

The author acknowledges the editorial support of Aurora LeMere.

ISBN 13: 978-1502586766,
10: 1502586762

First Edition published November 2012
Third Edition and First Print Copyright © 2014
All Rights Reserved

Dedicated to Cecelia Jacobson
who encouraged me over our 28 years of friendship
by saying, "You should write a book."

"At times the world can seem an unfriendly and sinister place but believe us when we say that there is much more good in it than bad. All you have to do is look hard enough... There are people who know that there is always a mystery to be solved, and they take comfort in... writing down any important evidence... What might seem like a series of unfortunate events may be the first steps of a journey..."

> From the screenplay "A Series of Unfortunate Events" based on the books of Limminy Snicket

Table of Content

Chapter 1, Day 4, Arrival..................Page 11
Chapter 2, Day 6, Shopping..................Page 13
Chapter 3, Day 10, In the Moment..................Page 15
Chapter 4, Day 21, Thanks and Praise..................Page 17
Chapter 5, Day 28, What to wear..................Page 19
Chapter 6, Day 29, Heart of Darkness..................Page 21
Chapter 7, Day 31, What to Eat..................Page 23
Chapter 8, Day 35, Oddities..................Page 26
Chapter 9, Day 36, Paying for Services..................Page 31
Chapter 10, Day 39, Can't Complain..................Page 33
Chapter 11, Day 42, House Buying..................Page 35
Chapter 12, Day 44, Weird Deal,..................Page 38
Chapter 13, Day 45, It's a Jungle..................Page 40
Chapter 14, Day 46, Just Can't Take It..................Page 42
Chapter 15, Day 50, Merry Christmas..................Page 44
Chapter 16, Day 52, Christmas Goose..................Page 47
Chapter 17, Day 52, Girls..................Page 50
Chapter 18, Day 57, Happy New Year..................Page 53
Chapter 19, Day 58, It Is So Loud..................Page 56
Chapter 20, Day 59, Ghosts of Friends..................Page 59
Chapter 21, Day 81, Making a Home..................Page 61
Chapter 22, Day 86, Everywhere I Go..................Page 63
Chapter 23, Day 87, I Am Psychic..................Page 65
Chapter 24, Day 93, Granada, Nicaragua..................Page 68
Chapter 25, Day 97, Quarterly Review..................Page 73
Chapter 26, Day 103, Valentine's Day..................Page 77
Chapter 27, Day 105, Foreign Culture..................Page 79
Chapter 28, Day 107, Loneliness..................Page 81
Chapter 29, Day 108, Hobbies..................Page 83
Chapter 30, Day 109, Food..................Page 85
Chapter 31, Day 115, Traveler's Sickness..................Page 87
Chapter 32, Day 118, Spare Change..................Page 89
Chapter 33, Day 119, Tico Spanish..................Page 92
Chapter 34, Day 121, Women..................Page 95

Chapter 35, Day 124, Money..................................Page 98
Chapter 36, Day 125, Tico Words......................Page 100
Chapter 37 Day 126, Business............................Page 102
Chapter 38, Day 129, Your Arrival......................Page 106
Chapter 39, Day 133, Pat and Mike....................Page 109
Chapter 40, Day 134, Living Gringo Style..................Page 111
Chapter 41, Day 136, Spiritual Experience................Page 114
Chapter 42, Day 140, Human Experience..................Page 117
Chapter 43, Day 141, Furniture Shopping.................Page 119
Chapter 44, Day 164, Culture Shock.....................Page 122
Chapter 45, Day 171, Green Season.......................Page 124
Chapter 46, Day 174, Luggage...........................Page 126
Chapter 47, Day 175, Housing...........................Page 128
Chapter 48, Day 178, Miracles............................Page 131
Chapter 49, Day 181, Social Life..........................Page 133
Chapter 50, Day 182, Love..............................Page 135
Chapter 51, Day 183, What to Bring.....................Page 137
Chapter 52, Day 187, Tico Time.........................Page 139
Chapter 53, Day 190, Botanical Gardens...................Page 141
Chapter 54, Day 192, Gringo Fantasy....................Page 143
Chapter 55, Day 196, Weather...........................Page 145
Chapter 56, Day 201, Retirement..........................Page 147
Chapter 57, Day 202, Feeling Gray.......................Page 150
Chapter 58, Day 205, Gardening and Cooking.............Page 152
Chapter 59, Day 212, Earthquakes........................Page 157
Chapter 60, Day 215, Tico Personality....................Page 160
Chapter 61, Day 217, Home Improvement.................Page 162
Chapter 62, Day 220, Security............................Page 165
Chapter 63, Day 221, Being a Foreigner...................Page 167
Chapter 64, Day 222, Stress..............................Page 169
Chapter 65, Day 245, David Panama   Page.171
Chapter 66, Day 246, Pirates of the Caribbean   Page 173
Chapter 67, Day 250, Grecia   Page 175
Chapter 68, Day 254, Metaphoric Life   Page 177
Chapter 69, Day 257, Woman's World....................Page 180
Chapter 70, Day 259, Studying Spanish...................Page 182

Chapter 71, Day 265, Friends..................................Page 184
Chapter 72, Day 268, My Birthday........................Page 186
Chapter 73, Day 274, Selfless Giving......................Page 189
Chapter 74, Day 275, Tico Directions.....................Page 192
Chapter 75, Day 278, Sometimes Depressing..........Page 195
Chapter 76, Day 285, Tico Business.......................Page 197
Chapter 77, Day 288, Tourist versus Resident.........Page 199
Chapter 78, Day 290, Dirt......................................Page 202
Chapter 79, Day 292, Kindness..............................Page 204
Chapter 80, Day 294, Personal Growth..................Page 206
Chapter 81, Day 296, Online Shopping..................Page 208
Chapter 82, Day 298, Talking Tico.........................Page 211
Chapter 83, Day 348, A Trip to the U.S.A...............Page 213
Chapter 84, Day 352, Tico Friendship....................Page 215
Chapter 85, Day 354, Laundry...............................Page 218
Chapter 86, Day 357, Pastimes..............................Page 221
Chapter 87, Day 360, Online Dating......................Page 223
Chapter 88, Day 361, Trick or Treat.......................Page 225
Chapter 89, Day 363, Zak on Zen..........................Page 228
Chapter 90, Day 365, Was It Worth It? ....Page 230
Epilogue..Page 233

PROLOGUE

When I think of refugees I think of starving people from poor countries all over the world wanting to go to the United States to look for work and make a better life. I never thought I would find myself in a group known as "refugees" but there I was, nearing retirement age in a country facing economic decline and not having taken the most prudent track in life. Though far from destitute, I was facing the unpleasant reality that I might not have either enough money in my investments or in the faltering Social Security system to support myself in one of the most affluent nations in the world.

Living in an affluent nation was a double edged sword. There might have been clean water, paved streets, street lights, plentiful supplies of inexpensive consumer goods and excellent medical services; however they all came at a cost. The City taxes attached to my water bill were three times the cost of the water. The County wanted a fair share of my income for the privilege of paying for a home on their turf.

That top notch medical service was also very costly and the option to insure myself against exorbitant medical costs in 2009 was expensive. I had no chronic health problems and I prayed I never would but a half-hour medical treatment for an infection cost me over $400 and that did not include the medications and loss of income from down-time.

So I decided to move south where the weather suited my clothes. I could not see paying heating and/or air-conditioning costs for the remainder of my life. I sought to go native, live cheap and improve the quality of my life but how and where to do that was something I did not know.

My research guided me to Costa Rica where my 2010 Dollars seemed like they would go farther than in the US. However in order to stretch those Dollars I would have to go without a car and I would have to invest a large portion of my savings into buying a house. Paying rent for an unfurnished house or apartment would drive my monthly costs up in an unpredictable and inflationary fashion.

Costa Rica was reported to have a high inflation rate and my fixed income might not sustain housing cost increases. My single life at $400 per month in 2010 has just less than doubled in my married life of 2014. Aside from inflation, supporting my wife has increased living costs. Also you must consider that $400 per month is a no-frills single life in a Spanish speaking country.

Another serious consideration about going native and living cheap is that the lifestyle you will have is not one lived by the "beautiful people." The first two editions of this book were subtitled "Adjusting to a Culture" and you must adjust if you are going from a somewhat middle class American lifestyle to a poorer class Latino lifestyle.

In 2014 I am acculturated and accustomed to the behavioral norms. I still walk everywhere and have had my share of unpleasant street experiences. However I would not have traded that for a chance to insulate myself from the Costa Ricans by driving everywhere and only frequenting those places where English is spoken.

This series of "Letters to the North" chronicles those street experience, and as much as possible, explains the financial and social aspects of my first year of living in Costa Rica on $400 per month.

CHAPTER 1, DAY 4, ARRIVAL

It was day four in Costa Rica when I started writing this book. First of all I had my departure date confused and left in a hurry on Wednesday. Having planned to leave on Thursday, I flew out of Portland Oregon on Wednesday, November 8, 2009. It had taken me eight months to close my 57 years of American life to become a reluctant transplant. Of course upon arrival my ride was not waiting for me. I was not expected and there was no contingency plan for my stupidity.

The luggage had surprisingly arrived intact. Even the breakable items all survived the baggage handlers and after being awake from 6:00 A.M. on Wednesday until 5:00 P.M. on Thursday I could not seem to find one piece of luggage that was lazily circling the nearly empty carousel.

Customs was a breeze. They overlooked all the potentially sellable or taxable items in the carefree and detached style is so typical in Costa Rica. Stepping outside I went to the curb hoping that my *Gringo* and *Tico* friends had received my last minute email attempts to update my travel plans. With the exception of one phone number I had no way to locate my planned landing pad, which was the house that John was renting in San Isidro de Grecia. I had met John on my previous trip and we seemed to hit it off so I planned to sublet from him in a 3 bedroom house he was renting.

Numerous calls by an independent taxi driver (who was trying to hustle me for a fare) only produced repeated opportunities to listen to voice mail messages in Spanish. I guessed I could have gone back to the hotel where I stayed in March and rented a room until contact was made. After five or ten minutes of "Oh let's wait and see" contact was made.

The room in the house was still available. John was home and someone to help was going to meet me in Grecia to get another taxi and to direct me to John's place in the hills outside of town. In my best *Tico* fashion I negotiated the driver's $40 request down to a $30 agreement for a $20 ride. I thought I was cool, and the weather was warm.

I had been awake for over 36 hours if you didn't count the hour I passed out on the second leg of the flight from Houston to San Jose. (Side note: the Houston Intercontinental Airport was much more user friendly than the Denver airport.) So of course a small fiesta seemed in order for my homecoming and all. Having a party with copious amounts of beer and smoking appropriately lasted until 1:00 in the morning. By then I had been awake for 44 hours.

The sun rose at five AM and the day warmed up quickly. The 250 pounds of luggage took most of my attention on Friday and there were still more things to put away, organize and move into my lovely room with the private bath. The house was on a ridge that afforded beautiful views, sunrises, garden space, hot and cold water, electricity, cable, phone and maybe internet some day. It was a little strange to accustom myself to washing dishes in cold water and "dialing in" the shower for a warm one. For $200 a month for my share of the rent I thought I could learn how to make it work.

Other features of country living were the scorpions and stinging caterpillars which could be a small nuisance and minimally required sandals or shoes when walking around. The following day was shopping day and the cost and inconvenience of arranging rides to and from town was offset by the serenity and quiet of the country setting. I figured I'd give it all some time and let the whole event of relocating sink in.

CHAPTER 2, DAY 6, SHOPPING

You could take the boy out of the culture but you couldn't take the culture out of the boy. Industry still suited me and household projects called for both time and attention. I limited myself to one project a day but managed to start more than one every day. Friday was unpacking and rewiring the hall light switch so that the switch no longer controlled the hall and the bedroom light. The Saturday trip to town was an all day event with socializing and taxies and planning an evening of entertainment for Flor, John's girlfriend.

The Saturday shopping trip to Grecia's farmers' market put Eugene Oregon's farmers' market to shame with fruits, veggies, meat, cheese, pies and bread galore. The rain held back until after the buying spree that took place under the covered walkways. The market area is dedicated to the two day a week event. Then the clouds arrived to dump their contents in fits and spurts in one hour and half-hour increments until finally the skies cleared to the quiet of the night.

At the house the sound of the heavy rain on the metal roof was calming, in a white noise kind of way, without radio, conversation or thoughts to be heard. The pattern of morning sun with temperatures rising to 77 degrees only to be cooled by afternoon rains was a winter that complimented my clothes and my personality. Ah, this was paradise. Though I heard I had just missed a stint of four straight days of rain.

On Sunday I spent an hour in the garden space turning over the clay, pulling up the vegetative matter and dodging the ants. This was followed by the switching of the beds project. I disassembled the single and bunk beds that where permanent installed inside each of the two bedrooms. Before the end of the day I had a single bed assembled and ready for sleeping in my room and the bunk bed in parts in the guest room.

Monday I turned the bunk turned into two beds and my bedroom door was closing only slightly better than it had before I had arrived. I went dry goods shopping in Grecia for wire, food, shower curtain, cup hooks, tacks and a water bottle to replace the one I left at the farmer's market. John looked for pants with a 36 inch inseam; however a 32 inch inseam was a tall *Tico*. (Costa Ricans were locally referred to as *Ticos*.)

Both trips to town involved withdrawing cash from a bank ATM, figuring out local transportation and endless attempts to bridge the communication gap with mixed results. The most memorable comment about communication was "You need-a to learn how to speak-a the Spanish" after John and I had made a valiant effort speaking the limited Spanish that we had. Also, there was an interesting exchange at a hardware store where we struggled to find the words for what we wanted and later discovered that the helpful clerk had better English skills than our Spanish skills. For me, though reportedly unnecessary, developing language skills will be the single most important acculturating factor.

Day six was a Tuesday morning in November of 2009 (and I mean morning; about 5:30) when I finally began writing about the last weekend. It was easy to wake up to the bright sky, 70 degree air and the call of distant roosters. Oddly enough this all somehow seemed comfortable and familiar. Early rising had been a daily occurrence with no mechanical or electrical assistance but I had no established routine other than coffee…..

CHAPTER 3, DAY 10, IN THE MOMENT

Day ten was a Saturday again? (Where did the time go...? I would like to tell you the time just slid by while drinking Cuba Libres and Imperial Beer while kicking with my homies on the beach wearing dark shades and watching the girls go by.) Wednesday, Thursday and Friday were lost days; lost in the milieu of public transportation and bureaucratic entanglements. My lacking in both Spanish language and social skills was becoming more obvious.

The first two of the above mentioned days were filled with two hour bus rides to San Jose and two hours back. There were fun filled walks in the sun on city streets as well as sitting and waiting to meet people who had more misinformation and miscommunication than at which you could shake a palm frond. I was both lost and late and I was feeling as uptight as a New York Lawyer.

In the end I was back on a bus back to the town of Grecia and from there I knew the connection to the shared rental in San Isidro de Grecia. Thursday's trip included a fascinating visit to the Banco Nacional. (Relying on a *Tica* translator was a tricky event! Can you imagine that the person assigned to processing a $60K deposit was unaware that a cashier's check was an unacceptable form of deposit and had never heard that the bank needed a routing number for a wire transfer?)

In Costa Rica, there seemed to be a prevailing philosophy of laxity. [Do you know that concept, exalted by gurus and philosophers of being in the moment? If it isn't happening right now and doesn't affect me personally: *Que me importa*? (That is important to me?) That all seemed well and good in a monastic or contemplative lifestyle, but can you tell me please, how did the wheels keep turning?] I was a lost soul with my American concepts and values in what seemed to be a land of mysteriously foreign logic.

Some people said that they were here without any Spanish language skills and I only imagined that they were here with an abundance of cash assets. [*Tico* friends can help you if you have a very even temperament and you can maintain an air of *quedar bien* (keeping the good) in all your interactions.] Assertiveness or expressions of frustration were not received well and only further delayed processes.

There was also the risk of loss and theft looming overhead. There were so many honest and helpful people here that the confidence players were hard to distinguish from the real deal. In *El Norte* if a stranger was overly helpful and friendly I could assume they wanted something or maybe I was being setup me up for a scam. So many people here were friendly outgoing and helpful that the scammers were hard to distinguish from the just plain old good folk.

Everything was sacred here and therefore nothing was sacred here. (This was one of the great paradoxes. Telling a whopping tale to cover your tail was more highly revered than competence.) I digress… Friday I made a couple bus trips to downtown Grecia to bum some toll free calls to the States. (Honorable mention needed to go out to my dear friend Sue, the guardian of my papers and assets, without whom this would have been an impossible task.) This would all have been impossible without the support of friends and business' in the States.

I was beginning to feel unprepared for this. Maybe I didn't know what I had gotten myself into. I was floundering in uncharted waters without adequate resources or skills!

CHAPTER 4, DAY 21,
THANKS AND PRAISE

Some would say I am not the easiest guy to get along with. I may be honest, loyal, generous, loving, daring and bright. Did I mention tactless? If you put all that together you might find yourself in front of me facing aspects of yourself you would rather not see.

So it went with the alcoholic chain smoking John. My own bedroom and bath turned out to be not as private as presented. John needed to control his surroundings including those he offered to relinquish or share. That was o.k. until it included cranking up the TV music late at night and having heavy drinking parties and smoking sessions outside my bedroom door.

I guess this was my second Costa Rica con job. The first was a credit card scam that forced me to change account numbers after signing up for my ARCR membership. With John I was out $345 in pre-paid rent. I might have been able to stick it out a little longer if I had not been suffering for a week from an infection in my leg. The doctor said abscess infections were common here in Costa Rica.

My leg had become swollen and I was quite sick from what appeared to be a spider bite that I received on day six. The redness had spread and a nasty black spot was growing. On day twelve I was beginning to get concerned. John called a friend who has been here on and off for 20 years and his suggestion was the public hospital. He must have never gone to the public hospital. True there was no cost for the examination, antibiotics and anti-inflammatory injection. However there had to be a better source for medical care than the public hospital. As interesting as they were I spared you the hospital stories. I will only say that the conditions were less than sterile and the treatment less than satisfactory.

By day 16 I had moved out of the house in San Isidro down to a hotel in Grecia Central and began my first real medical attention. I stayed at same hotel where I stayed in March 2009 and the people there were very nice. I was paying $300 a month for a large room with 2 double beds, tiled floors, tongue and groove ceiling, kitchen appliances and a tiled shower. Paying $300 there felt better than paying $200 for "half" of $350 a month rent.

I was not worrying too much about money or housing when I thought I might lose my leg or life. The day I moved I found a new *Doctora* who spoke English. Thankfully she had access to medications that were not available in the hospital. The strong antibiotics gave me next to the worst case of dry heaves I had experienced in my life. (The only worse condition was caused by a tiny tasting of Polk Salad at age 27 when living in Ukiah, California. The highly toxic plant, the root of which resembled Jerusalem artichoke, caused five hours of heaves and was only stopped by medication in a hospital.) The antibiotic nausea only lasted four hours and stopped on its own.

The *Doctora* and clinic staff were helpful, honest, knowledgeable and affordable by US standards. I had lost a week or so but the wound was healing and I felt I was in competent young caring hands. I hung out in the hotel and tried to heal from a combination of infection and head cold. It was healthier at the Healthy Day Apt & Hotel since there was no one chain smoking outside my door.

I decided that living in the country was no longer an option. Now I preferred to look for a house closer to the city center. The temperature in town was just right. There were too many nasty bugs in the country; and there were fewer in town and the lack of bird life was proportional. I was very grateful for the good medical attention and the quiet smoke free place to be. I hoped everyone had as wonderful a Thanksgiving Day as I had on that rainy Thursday in 2009.

CHAPTER 5, DAY 28, WHAT TO WEAR

Day 28 brought the beginning of December and I welcomed the waning moon. (Somehow the passing of the full moon always seemed to be more pleasing than the approaching of the full moon for me.) *La Doctora* wanted me to stay on light duty until the next Monday because of the leg infection. I continued resting by watching old American television and movies with Spanish subtitles so I could learn a little and do even less. Lucky for me I missed all those years of T.V. so it was all new to me.

Those early days in Grecia were a great journey of self discovery and I presumed the challenges were there to test my resolve and would pass quietly away through the process of acclimation. I was in a big learning curve and there was much to learn. Aside from the language and the culture there was the whole aspect of understanding other people. Sometimes I just didn't "get IT."(You know what I mean?)

In the States we were all the same somehow; people were easier to "read." Little was as it appeared to be here. Perhaps this was supposed to be a spiritual awakening to the illusion of life… (How Zen!) People really seemed to be in the moment here and what "was" in one moment was no longer in the next. It was that same fluidity that permeated the air and was the reason it took two days in the sun at 75 plus degrees to dry socks. It did not feel humid; but it smelled humid every now and then in certain spots.

More guys were seen in town in shorts and caps than I remembered from my earlier visit and sunglasses seemed more common than they had been nine months earlier. Women wore anything from business suits to short-shorts. Some were scantily clad while others were modestly dressed. The most common trend in ladies wear was skin tight, low cut and high heeled. The sun was a likely issue for *Gringas*, but women's wear had far fewer constraints than men's wear.

Other than the intense sun one had to contend with the occasional downpour. I had not seen a long rain spell since I had arrived and the locals carried umbrellas on threatening days. Just like Oregon the weather went from bright to cloudy to rainy and back to bright in the matter of an hour. I read that a light rain shell was recommended for the cloud forest but I think almost anywhere you go it will be warm. I was glad to have picked up a high end collapsible umbrella in the States.

I was eternally grateful for the mosquito net I was gifted. The bugs were not "bad" in town but I preferred to avoid the buzzing in my sleep and the irksome itches. I had also pre-treated travel clothes with repellant available from a camping store. Everyone would like to visit the jungle, cloud forest and beaches and that meant encountering more serious bugs than I had seen in Grecia. When looking at my leg wound the *medicos* all asked me if I had been bitten in one of the tropical jungle beach areas where the toxic insects seemed to reside. It was the same in Oregon. (Try camping out in the woods and wait for the bugs to discover your locale; they did.)

What you should bring for a visit to Costa Rica are clothes made of: silk, linen, microfiber, light cotton and polyester. It was hard to remember that I was at 3,600 feet and only ten degrees above the equator. The sun was bright and men usually wore long pants and short-sleeved shirts, however the local had dark skin. I needed a hat and arm covering. I usually lounged on the hotel grounds in shorts and a short-sleeved shirt and then I changed clothes for walking in town.

(By all means you should bring everything you might want to have during a stay because you might not find it here or it might seem prohibitively expensive to buy at Costa Rican prices. A few goods were cheaper but I wouldn't count on availability when it comes to finding something you want or something in your size.)

CHAPTER 6, DAY 29, HEART OF DARKNESS

By day 29 the *La Doctora* said I needed to spend two to three hours a day sunning my gauze covered lesion. I was still a White boy in a country of brown folk. I could only take an hour of sun at a time and needed sunscreen to keep from getting sunburned. One day while lying out under the dappled shade of the palms something interesting happened:

I felt a small thud on the front of my pure white shirt and saw that two small black bugs had fallen out of the palms in the throes of a battle to the death. A quick flick and the two continued their rumble in the jungle on the tiled pool deck. They were of the same species and I found that strangely disturbing. For a while I felt like the fictional Col. Kurtz from Conrad's Heart of Darkness watching a snail slither over the cutting edge of a razor. Uninterested in watching brother fight brother, I thoughtlessly looked in a different direction for awhile as my sole occupation was to dry the wound that would not heal.

[Hunter S. Thompson's (the 60's, 70's rogue writer for Rolling Stone magazine) has nothing on me. He might be dead but I was still railing against the wind. He was resting in peace but I was tearing up the sheets in my sleep. "The horror, the horror." said Col. Kurtz.]

I was bored to my wits end. I would have liked to have used the pool, spa, weight room and tennis or basketball courts. I missed taking the early morning walks I had taken on my last visit. I had too much down time and my mind was playing tricks on me. All but four of my days here in Costa Rica were spent dealing with the bite turned infection. I healed slowly enough and in this moisture I was healing even slower. I was ready to do something.

When I looked back at the bugs an ant was carrying away the dead one. The survivor, if there was one, was gone. That bug event and an email from a cousin had me thinking about blood relatives and family dysfunction. It seemed that the only way to make sense of familial strife was to leave logic out of the equation. I couldn't make sense out of the senseless. I couldn't understand the snail surviving the unfathomable by thinking in normal terms.

I kept thinking of an ad I saw on the television about an interview with the Buddha. The interviewer asked the Buddha if he made mistakes. The Buddha replied that he was making a mistake right then. I felt equally as flawed as any Buddha and all this seemed like a mistake. Like the Buddha I had little choice but to do what I did. Perhaps it was the best that I could do. If I could have done more or better I would have. (Wouldn't you? Who amongst you wouldn't like to be greater in terms of compassion, love, faith, hope...?)

This also applied to looking inwardly. I couldn't look at myself and see anything. It had to not be the "me" that was looking to be able to see anything. I was limited in my abilities due to some misconstrued impression that I knew something. My friend Randy said it best when he said that whenever "he" made a choice "he" made the wrong choice. The thought that I was completely and unequivocally inadequate to trust my own thoughts seemed an incredible discovery.

CHAPTER 7, DAY 31, WHAT TO EAT

On day 31, I wondered if no one knew about Robert Conrad's book Heart of Darkness about the Vietnam War (movie: Apocalypse Now). Had no one heard of that crazy contract journalist Hunter S. Thompson who became a raging alcoholic and heavy drug user and went on assignment and wrote about anything other than fight or race he was sent to cover? No one remembers Doonesbury's Duke? Fear and Loathing in Las Vegas? Well, movie goers and intellectuals were a dying breed in the good old USA.]

Well, I went to the *Feria* (farmers' market) again on Saturday for my weekly ration of fresh veggies. My *Tica* friend said this was the best *Mercado* in all of Costa Rica. The Friday and Saturday market had beautiful avocados five for a dollar eighty, lettuce for 70 cents, brown eggs three dollars for 18, broccoli, green onions, green beans, limes, bananas, oranges, and carrots that rounded out the bulk of my shopping. I tended to be a creature of habit, and I bought the same groceries each time with no attempt to try the new and unusual produce that did abound.

I must comment on the *Gringo* baker, *Buen Pan Tomas* of Atenas who brought beautifully rich whole grain breads and sweet goods to the *Feria*. The small, but heavy loaf was three dollars, but worth every penny. Store bought air puffed loafs of bread were cheaper. The Maxi Bodega was the new Wal-Mart spawned grocery/department store of Grecia and was considered part of a "mall." At the Maxi I bought a small whole barbecued chicken for about seven dollars and fifty cents, a block of cheese for three dollars and kefir for about three dollars. This all seemed not too expensive by US standards.

Most *Tico* cheese was sour but I had found more mild flavored cheeses. I also found Cheddar, Gouda and other American style cheeses. (But, that was where food got expensive.) Ten to twelve bucks for a six-pack of beer, four dollars for a bag of chips; and soda, ice cream, salad dressings, even canned tuna cost more than their stateside counterparts. If I could live on fresh foods alone then grocery shopping was affordable. If I wanted to live like an American I needed to be prepared to find life here more expensive than in the US However, the chicken soup I made that day was as good as any I had made in the States and cost me less to make.

Nutritional power was not the only power to think about. Another oddity was the electricity. (I had not checked the voltages, but I suspected the voltages here varied.) Nothing was grounded and plug adapters were a must for all the two pronged outlets. Motors seemed to work harder here and my magic bullet blender started to smell bad with very little use. Items that ran through transformers like rechargeable items and computers seemed to function better, but the amount of time a charge could be held seemed to suffer. Also, my rechargeable batteries seemed to wear out prematurely.

Lightening storms also posed a risk to electrical components. With little to no grounding a high electrical charge in the air could ruin your equipment. An overcurrent protection strip might help a little but I wouldn't rely on it. Unplugging electronics seemed to be the only sure protection.

On another business note I rented a P.O. Box. My *Tica* friend earned a whopping one dollar and eighty cents (one hours pay) for bringing me to the PO and helping me fill out the forms and explaining the contract. It cost three dollars a year for the box but it cost about $20 to buy the rights to rent the box. (That took a little time to sink into my thick head. I needed to go back in January to pay for the next year's rent.)

Generally people cannot order anything substantial from the US Import tariffs make receiving ordered goods prohibitively expensive. Anything other than a letter or a gift might cost more in import tax than price that was paid for the item.

Import tariffs and regulations varied constantly and getting reliable information was also difficult. The box remained almost unused for the entire year. One of the two letters that were sent to me never made it. I worry about the security of mail here in Costa Rica.

CHAPTER 8, DAY 35, ODDITIES

Wednesday December 9 was day 35 of my adventure and my "tropical ulcer" was healing well after 19 days of antibiotics and daily cleaning and topical treatments. I was feeling much better on day 29 as the three inch wide gap that was one inch deep had filled to a two inch gap; one quarter inch deep and the inflammation had subsided. The worst was behind me and I would not detail the final aspects of the healing process.

Figuring out how to bandage the lesion was my greatest health care concern. Too much adhesive had taken its toll on the adjoining skin. It was a drag to be getting older and healing so much slower. I had not felt well enough to start seriously studying my Rosetta stone program but I had been listening to the audio refresher. I wanted to plug the program as I had only completed level one and the locals were very impressed with my Spanish. (I can only imagine how conversant I will be when I have completed the program.) I bought all five levels but I recommend level one for anyone traveling south. After three levels I should be almost conversational. The study was time consuming and took effort but it was magic in terms of retention.

That TV ad of an "interview" with the Buddha also said: "when you stop making mistakes you stop being." There was also a clip from Pirates of the Caribbean on TV promoting the upcoming showing of the movie… "Take all you can. Give nothing in return." That was the only line in the commercial and it aired at least hourly. (I wondered if this ad appealed to the national psyche and give an intimate glance into the national mind-set?)

I thought I was doing a fair job of objective reporting. However some friends had responded that my writing looked like despair, depression, and unhappiness. I felt that was a result of misinterpretation by my editorial friends in the north. Most people didn't understand my weirdness. I guessed that's why I was here in Costa Rica and they were still there in the US

A common expression and salutation here was *Pura Vida* (pure life). This is a sacred place like a spiritual vortex. I felt that the land and the people had been touched by God. I would rather die here trying to make this new life work than to live up there in the hinterlands in my old familiar ways.

So many Northerners had the illusion that moving to a tropical paradise relieving a person of the duties, responsibilities and the efforts needed to live. I hated telling people in the US I was going to Costa Rica because I could see in their faces the fantasy that moving there would mean the end of all my worries in life. It was easy to confuse vacationing with living. (My recommendation to the meek among you…"Don't get off the boat." Just stay on that ship and look at the emerald coastline from afar. On board you can gorge yourselves on greasy sugary foods and be with people who look, speak, think and act like you do.)

I would have commented on the weather but it had been the same every day. I hadn't seen a drop of rain in two weeks and it was 75 to 85 degrees daily and in the 60's overnight but sometimes the sky clouded up in the afternoon. That day I went to town in the afternoon and was caught in a downpour. (I had just said that it hadn't been raining so there it was… rain.) In town, I met a guy at an electrical supply place who spoke English very well and he brought me to two other hardware stores and asked for a sink stopper for me. He was just a great friendly fellow who wanted to help a *Gringo* in need but they just don't have sink stoppers here.

It was hard to realize that Christmas was coming. They hung icicle lights on the chalet style roof line of the hotel. The Christmas lights seemed an oddity with the palm treed borders and warm weather. However, there was a little bit of Christmas everywhere. Small plastic trees and discrete light displays could be seen in many places. I regretted missing the orchid exposition that had been in Grecia while I was still on light duty.

I was saving my legwork for house shopping and I had started to make inquiries in earnest. I had talked with Realtors and I knew the best deals would have been found walking around town looking for *se vende* (for sale) signs. Cheap housing in Grecia seemed to be around sixty thousand dollars and not the thirty thousand dollars I had previously been led to believe. I had just started to look and more research was needed to really understand the market. I met my first Realtor. If you thought Realtors were like used car sales people up north then you can only imagine how cutthroat they were here. Costa Rican Realtors, listings and sales were completely unregulated.

As of my last trip to San Jose all my paperwork for the immigration application had been completed. I really had money in the bank here and had five years of *Colones* (local cash) coming to me from my own investment of dollars. Now it seemed that touring homes was a realistic pursuit. I saw dumps, fixers, finished homes and some that I even considered livable.

A beautiful home in San Roque was not selling for some reason. It seemed worth the $60,000.00 price tag compared to some of the fixers I saw. I questioned why someone put so much money into a remodel and then want to move? The adjoining place was for sale and had sewage problems... their downhill neighbor had cut into their septic line and refused to grant an easement for a new septic tank.

The six houses that one Realtor had listed in my price range were between twenty seven and sixty one thousand dollars. The twenty seven thousand dollar house was the one with the septic issues and a bunch of broken windows. The further away from central Grecia a house was the less expensive it was. A ninety square meter house close to central Grecia was reportedly only ten years old and had one wall that joined the neighbor's dwelling. It had an asking price of forty six thousand and was the only house we could not get inside to see. That house was in the south of town overlooking a soccer field on a quiet street and faced west. That meant the back yard, if there was one, would be shaded in the afternoon.

(This brought me to the whole issue of orientation. Nothing was more disconcerting to a person with a good sense of direction than to not be able to tell which way was north. I thought this disorientation was caused by the sun being so high in the sky. What made matters worse was that the sun moved from a southern to a northern orientation. My sense of direction was completely gone. I had to rely on landmarks for orientation.)

Another oddity that occurred here was in the water. I didn't know how this could be but the water appeared thicker here. (You know how water ripples when you pour it into a stainless pot?) Here the waves seemed further apart and seemed to move slower and the water had a strong magnifying effect. I had observed the effects of the water often because I had begun boiling my drinking water.

A Funny story I was told by the Doctor that runs a travel clinic in Eugene Oregon: the only time he got Giardiasis was from a Colorado municipal system that just happened to be shut down when he spent the night in that town. He recommended iodine treatment and secondarily he recommended boiling.

No one treats their water here and I have never heard of anyone having trouble from water borne disease. I had started boiling drinking water because of the antibiotics I had been taking and the resulting lack of good intestinal. I drank yogurt but still didn't trust my gut to fight off a little bug.

I had to boil water for the daily cleaning of my leg wound so I made it a big pot full and cooled the rest for drinking. Except for coffee, I eventually took to drinking bottled water and later returned to boiling my drinking water.

CHAPTER 9, DAY 36, PAYING FOR SERVICES

On day 36 I was busy again. I saw three more houses that day. The thirty eight thousand dollar house was a real fixer. The Realtor said it would sell fast. (Fat chance!) I guessed it was going to take closer to $55K to get a nice small place close to downtown. The areas that had houses I really liked were the most expensive.

There was a learning curve with house shopping as well. Real estate sales do not work the same here as they do up north. I had read that incorporating was the safest way to own and sell property. The details of buying, selling and incorporation were hard to understand. I had found a Realtor who spoke English which was a real plus. Yesterday's guy spoke no English. Kira, my *Tica* friend, had to help me. She was helpful but was young and had no business experience. We spent three hours looking at places online and in person. I spoke with her in English and she translated; she and the Realtor talked extensively. When I asked "What did he say?" she replied that he was just chatting with her.

The economy was also depressed here. I had heard that in 2008 there were two closings a week and in 2009 there was only one closing a month. Just like up north people thought their houses were worth more than they were the year before. However buyers were fewer and farther between. I saw the insides of eight or more places all together. Unfortunately there were no MLS or unified home listings or appraisals of home values.

I saw the insides of a couple more places and was pretty sure the fifty thousand dollar place would work best for me. That wouldn't leave much of a financial buffer but it seemed like it was ready to live in and the house was suppose to come furnished. The downside was there was no porch from which to greet the neighbors.

There was still one house I wanted to see on the inside and it could save me ten grand and was closer to central and it had a porch to sit on. The downside was that the wall was joining a very noisy neighbor's house.

On the topic of money, I tallied up my medical expenses for the three weeks of treatment. The entire medical treatment only cost me around $150 to $175. I thought this was a far cry better than the $400 I spent on one Doctor's visit in Oregon for a similar problem.

On a related topic, I also went to a Dentist even though I didn't have any mouth problems. However, since I was full of antibiotics I figured it would be a good time to have my teeth cleaned. The Dentist was over a half hour late to his first appointment of the day with me. (*Tico* time!) The cleaning took over an hour and was $36, and he said he discovered a small cavity which he filled for another $36. I had to hurry from the dentist office to meet a Realtor so there was no time to verify the cavity. This was a bargain by US standards but I still wondered if there was really a cavity there or if it was just "make-work."

I've been very happy with the private medical care I received and I can probably afford to pay out-of-pocket for any medical attention short of a major surgery. If I needed major surgery or continuous medications I would look at either insurance or funeral plans. I have since donated my corporal remains to a Costa Rican medical university to be used for training and research.

CHAPTER 10, DAY 39, CAN'T COMPLAIN

Day 39 was a Sunday. Saturday shopping and soup making had typically been followed by Sunday cleaning. It was noon when I wrote and the laundry was finished and the hotel's refrigerator had been dismantled, defrosted and cleaned with bleach water. The hotel cleaning staff had a different hygiene standard than you find in the states. My thoughts that day had been on the cultural thinking of the Costa Rican people.

[If you can, look at my writings not as complaints but try and see this as reporting. Many readers see these stories as problems or complaints (The American Way) and cannot elevate their thoughts to consider that this was all just something for me to learn, a new way of thinking and another culture to which I am adjusting.]

When walking down the sidewalk I regularly came up behind *Ticos* due to my relatively long legged stride. Most commonly, if there was more than one, they would spread out to take the whole walkway and then slowed their pace. The funniest of all was when I came up upon a woman who suddenly started to weave back and forth on the sidewalk. I would start to pass on the right and she weaved over to the right. When I started to pass on the left she would swerve to the left. My uncontrolled laughing out loud embarrassed her into keeping to one side. What can I say, it struck me as funny!

When driving, *Ticos* swerved toward pedestrians. Not to hit them but as if to say, "You better pay attention because I am more important than you are because I have a car." If walking across a street or driveway I found that drivers will block the path and make pedestrians walk around their car even though they cannot proceed due to cross traffic. These same blocking techniques were also used on fellow drivers.

When I was in a Realtor's car and we were about to make a three point turn in a "T" intersection a taxi drove into the "T". He stopped his car and stepped out to check his gas cap. Then, he stepped back into his car and proceeded straight down the street he had just pulled off.

My least favorite car ploy was leaving cars running. I did not care about the gas or the pollution. What irked me was that drivers would back up to my open hotel room door and idle their exhaust into my room. There were many noisy cars here and the racket right outside the open door and windows was a bit annoying. God bless my bad language skills because there was nothing I could say about any of this. I just closed the door and windows and then vacated the room and waited to clear the air later.

When I was buying lettuce in the farmers market I was short changed two cents. (Who would complain? It is not *Tico* to comment about shortchanging.) It was considered impolite to complain about others stealing from you. This was especially true as a *Gringo* because *Gringos* were perceived as having unlimited wealth. There was just something about being taken advantage of that made me take pause.

I learned that the best approach was to bring exact change and get good at counting the odd coinage (there were three different "dimes" and two different "nickels"). Short changing and overcharging was most common when breaking a big bill or large coin. It was not that I was being hurt financially but it left me feeling rather stupid. For some reason I wanted to feel smart; or, at least, I wanted to feel like I was not a fool.

(Perhaps *Ticos* were an impotent people? Did the years of being downtrodden show up in passive aggressive behavior? Being late, keeping others waiting, pulling one over on another and getting in the way seemed to be very common. However, I don't forget there were many of very sweet and helpful people as well.)

CHAPTER 11, DAY 42, HOUSE BUYING

It was a Wednesday on day 42 and the female personality here was something to note. How funny that my female cousin emailed me to warn me about female Realtors. Women here were much different than women in the north. There was a Madonna image that was culturally engendered here. This does not change the promiscuous mentality or the employment dominance of men, but it does create a mindset in the women.

(I shouldn't even start with the Realtor.) The Realtor would and did say anything to try to close the sale quickly. I wished I could have described all the prater she produced in order to sell me on each and every house we viewed. Some of those houses I would not have even considered staying in for an hour; never mind spending a night or 30 years. She would go on and on at each place with "you could" and "all you have to do." I was thinking; "How could I get out of here while maintaining an appearance of sociability and civility?" That social and polite appearance was very important here and I could not afford to offend the Realtor. She might know someone I would need help from later and her bad word could cost me dearly. I might want something from her, like a referral for workers, and hurt feelings could leave her not liking me.

She was who I had to work with and we were moving forward on the $55,000.00 house. The asking price was down from 60 or 65 or 75 (all of which the Realtor said). They also said the asking price did not include a commission for my Realtor. The seller accepted my fifty thousand dollar offer. Between the Rentista and this house my proceeds from the house sale in Oregon were spent. That meant $110,000 for 5 years income and a place to live.

Costa Rican women did not complain or ask for much here. They did, however, have very strong opinions and were not shy about stating them. My poor Realtor was biting her lip as I questioned the liens on the property which she insisted did not matter. At first the Realtor claimed there were no liens on the property. However, I could see there were three different documents referenced against the title of the property. She also kept telling me I didn't need an attorney and that she knew that the title was clear. Two *Gringo* guys in her office and I batted around what the liens might mean and how to have the documents reviewed by an attorney. I felt sorry for her as I could see in her eyes that she thought her Christmas bonus (large commission) was going out the window. Costa Ricans, in general, were not much for delayed gratification which was another reason they were a poor people.

At the lawyers, it cost $350 for the corporation papers and $100 for the power of attorney. There was at least another grand in closing fees and I was waiting to learn exactly how much. All together it cost at least $55,000 to move into the home. That left me a small chunk of cash outside the Rentista money for an emergency, house furnishings or a shopping trip to the US. These numbers will not be valid by the time you are ready to move here as immigration requirements change and Costa Rica was experiencing thirty percent inflation.

The house was a 10 minute walk from the center of town in a quiet neighborhood. It was a livable space that I had to check out completely. It came with some furnishings, and I was scheduled to have possession on January 5, 2010. Most unfurnished houses here had only walls, floors and a roof and no cabinets, closets or appliances were included; if the electric and plumbing worked it was a plus.

All the other houses less than $60K were total projects. Those houses were not just cosmetic fixers, but rather, broken in some way and/or unfinished. Homes close to town were twice the price of homes outside of town. I crunched all the numbers on all the houses; price per sq ft, lot size, livability, neighborhood and needed repairs and I felt that this was a fair deal. It was not a great deal but it was a fair deal. I could have waited for another deal but this one was "here and now" and it felt and seemed good enough. Perfect, after all, was the enemy of good.

CHAPTER 12, DAY 44, WEIRD DEAL

Day 44 brought the story of the Realtor from… I don't know where. Some people here really did have a different mentality and there were no holds barred. The negotiations seemed normal in the beginning. (Remember, nothing was as it appeared and I could not look at things through any normal perspective.) In the end, I was confused and amazed that things could be so weird.

The house I liked had been for sale for six months for either: 75, 65, or 60 Thousand. The price was now Fifty five Thousand according to my Realtor. By crunching the numbers on the comparable homes for sale Fifty Thousand seemed reasonable. An offer was made to my Realtor and presumably made to the seller's agent. The Realtor said the seller wanted to split the difference and was asking for $52,500. My Spanish was not good enough to work directly with the selling agent or the seller. So I waited a day or two. This was the nicest house I had seen close to the center of town in my price range.

I told the agent to proceed and I spoke to the broker hoping to reduce the commission. The broker confirmed my assumption that the selling price was $50,000 and the $2,500 was an extra commission on top of the $5,000.00 (ten percent) commission the seller paid. I was happy I saved a little and scheduled time to thoroughly check the house for functionality. Everything checked out except a stacked switch in which the outlet was not working. The electrical panel checked out, all the water and drains worked, the roof drain was clear all the way to the street and the septic was accessible albeit in the laundry/shop. The only obviously needed repair was the galvanized roof which required repainting to prevent further rusting. All in all, this was a livable, serviceable and comfortable place.

We went to the attorney's office to begin the earnest agreement and I had the $1,800 earnest money in hand. The seller's lawyer needed to review the contract and my lawyer needed time to write it. We were scheduled to return at 3 PM. Then, it starts becoming laughable. The agent picked me up and was very upset that her dog was having an epileptic fit and might die and was now at the vets being treated. She explained to me there was a change in the procedure and I could save attorney fees by filling out the papers at the broker's office. She kept telling me the attorney was unnecessary and the buying procedure was different in Costa Rica. Her English wasn't that great and I thought that when we arrived in the broker's office one of the American brokers would explain.

One broker said he did not know what was happening but that he would personally guarantee my deposit. The other broker had nothing to say and the agent was struggling to translate the contract. I understood most of the boilerplate words in context, except the ownership transferred between the seller and the broker. My money was with the attorney and I was supposed to sign off my rights to the home and the agent was trying to assure me that was normal. (Maybe the broker was planning to take possession of the house and sell it to another buyer. Maybe I would have recovered my $1,800, with a struggle. Worst of all, I could have transferred the $52.5K to the attorney's account and ended up buying the house for the broker.)

The good news was that a little voice in my head said "no, no, no" and I insisted on going back to the attorney. In the attorney's office: the selling price was $50,000 and not $52,500; and I had a written agreement signed by the seller's agent, and; we were scheduled to close on January 4.

If not for my intuition, I could have lost the house and $52.5K and have been financially devastated. That was not an uncommon Latin American story.

CHAPTER 13, DAY 45, IT'S A JUNGLE

Day 45 saw me frustrated and confused and feeling insecure and this all made me a little irritable. Gee…there were only so many people in the world to whom I was supposed to disclose that kind of personal information. (This was a rant that I hoped was at least entertaining?) My need for security continued to rage. I supposed I needed the audience and maybe not the approval nor the help, but the audience to validate the reality of my experience. (Do you know that old saying about the tree falling in the forest?)

Living here really messed with my head. When you add in the frustration factor of foreign living it made me batty and irritable. (Here you go: You're a stranger in a foreign country, you have some language difficulties and your vision and hearing have deteriorated by this time in life. Those were just the ground rules and let's assume that this was an above average to good starting point.) I found out that this is just part of a normal six week depression cycle that happens to expatriates.

Now, imagine that no native person could give you directions to where you wanted to go, and any two native people would give you conflicting directions. People from my own culture who had been places also could not give me directions. Words like behind, in front, parallel, perpendicular, north, south, east, west, close, far, right, left, by and away from were seldom used correctly. (Personally, I wondered if I had landed in a country of alcoholics.)

I may be sharp but not that far above the norm. I would either have to change, adapt, and conform or perish trying. (My cousin thought I had this under control. (You do not control Costa Rica; Costa Rica controls you.) It's a jungle down here. It is a jungle here both literally and figuratively. It is not just a figure of speech. It was either eat of be eaten.) However, I had the solution to the bad real estate dealings.

I hired another lawyer to keep the questionable lawyer honest. The first lawyer I hired was recommended by the misleading Realtor who would have been happy to take advantage of me. I didn't know until after the fact that she was untrustworthy. I wanted to believe in the good of people. It really knocked me for a loop when I lost my trust in those people whom I was counting on for guidance and support. It wasn't really about <u>them</u>, it was about me and how it made me feel and what I could or could not do about it.

Also, I met a young man who said his purpose in life was helping others. He did massage and tried to sell real estate. He connected me to some great places (not listed and with no signs out front). He had a good take on the vibe of different areas but he was a little greedy or naive in trying to price houses. Remember that he was looking for a percent commission and (like a good salesman) wanted me to spend the most I could.

I use to say on the trade show circuit, "If I didn't get you to spend all the money in your pocket I was not doing a good job." (I was in the sporting firearms trade for ten years. It is a real sport: Olympics, clubs, competitions, target shooting, hunting and killing beer cans.)

He also brought me around town and introduced me to three women. He said he wanted to introduce me to some friends and they all turned out to be women who ran shops. The good news was that the beauty shop gal's brother was interested in selling his home in a very desirable location. I asked my friend if he was trying to find a *Gringo* boyfriend for these gals and he said, "Yes."

(Was that "Yes," I don't understand the question, or "Yes" I am trying to hook up these gals? Maybe he was trying to entice me to buy into their shops, or maybe, they were working girls, if you know what I mean.)

CHAPTER 14, DAY 46, JUST CAN'T TAKE IT

(What was it, Day 46?) My feelings were going from bad to worse. I was becoming incapable of hiding my angst under the façade of *Quidar Bien* (the national moral standard of keeping good). Unlike up north, there was not social permission to be anything other than jovial here in Costa Rica. It was more like a southern mentality here... mess with whoever you want just smile while you were doing it and keep smiling if you were the one being messed with. You could do likewise to them later with a smile on your face.

It was also a national pastime here to put one over on the *Gringo*. It was not bad enough that the hotel cleaning people had a hundred excuses for failing to clean the room or that they were helping themselves to my belongings. They started coming to my door to use the microwave. That is OK once or twice but every day and just walking into my open door without asking to be invited in?

I was cleaning my own room and that meant washing the towels and sheets along with my clothes. I really didn't mind. I liked having control of the soap and bleach content of the wash and I liked to dry laundry in the sun after taking some of the moisture out in the gas dryer. To me it made the clothes and linens fresher and cleaner. I went out to the clothesline every twenty minutes to turn them on the line and one day the towels and sheets that I had washed, dried and hung with my clothes were taken by the cleaning gal.

Of course, it was the same gal who could not help me clean because she had to drink coffee and then she needed to take all the cleaning tools I was using. It was also she who just walked into my room unannounced after using the microwave once to use the microwave again. I said, "No." and she wanted me to explain why she could not just use my kitchen as her own. All this was on top the attorney/money concern, and I started to feel like a helpless case.

[Yea, yea, yea; centering, relaxation, inner guides, what's the worst and detached attachment all sounded good but I wasn't there that week. I just didn't do well with high stress situations and I probably needed to look at the seasonal history factors as well. I was completely friendless here. Not that I had any really tight close friends in the States. (It was sad watching those profiler type crime shows. I considered myself lucky I was not a serial killer, child molester or sadistic kidnapper.) Lucky me, I just acted like a jerk sometimes.]

Anyway, Christmas was historically difficult for me. Too many unfulfilled expectations? Too much parental partying? Too much sugar? Too many rules about how to enjoy the holiday? Maybe I was just a pinhead from birth? Spoiled? Undisciplined? Genetically defective? I always liked to point to my alcoholic parentage and the wild and unpredictable actions by people who I relied on for safety and stability.

Whatever it was, it was mine now, and I was having some serious doubts about my ability to make it work here. I thought there was a virus in my computer because weird things happened while typing. People were unable to email me or even reply to my sent emails. My mood was horrible and my writing suffered.

I sure would miss the weather here. (I was thinking I could have started looking for places that were hiring electricians in the states.) Maybe I could have found an unlicensed State or one with reciprocation. Then, I could go and mess up in English. I didn't know that I would have wanted to return to Oregon. I would not have been fond of cold winters after experiencing a brief retirement here.

CHAPTER 15, DAY 50, MERRY CHRISTMAS

Day 50 was Christmas Eve day; Peace on Earth Goodwill toward men. Discrete lighting behind barred porches brightened or adjoined the small plastic trees adorned with assorted ornaments. So unlike their garish northern counterparts they were still an important event here in Costa Rica. Perhaps the daily brilliance of the equatorial sun illuminating an azure sky bursting with moisture droplets were all the lights you really needed. (The sky's so bright; I gotta wear shades, with UVA and UVB blockers.)

The Nativity in the Mall was lacking the Holy Child and awaited the miracle of the virgin birth. The next day would find the manger filled with the babe in swaddling clothes. As in many Latin countries, this day was the day people ran to the stores after work to find what Santa would be bringing the family. Many stores were open late that day, filled with frantic shoppers. When I was in Playa Del Carmen Mexico for Christmas a local told me the merchants raised all their prices for Christmas Eve Day because of the captive buyers.

Christmas here was similar to Mexico. Many people shopped Christmas Eve and all the merchants raised their prices for the event. Tamales were the Christmas meal here. It was summer-like weather. This Christmas talk seemed out of place. No excuses for seasonal affective disorder and I was glad to leave all that behind.

Costa Rica was filled with red and green year round as corrugated metal housetops that were painted adobe red had palms towering over their rouged roofs. Likewise, the Christmas spirit could be seen year round in the happy helpful people who greet you on the street or assist you without hesitation. A genteel spirit existed here in those of the rural mentality. They were just good old country folk that were happy to have another day to share with their neighbors.

Amongst my stories of challenge and frustration there was a Doctor who worked on me for 20 plus days out of the goodness of her heart. A *Gringo* drove 15 minutes to town and waited with me for an hour in the bank just to ask some questions on my behalf. This same *Gringo* then drove me to his attorney's office to make an introduction and waited 15 minutes while she worked on my papers. A total stranger walked me around town to help me find a sink stopper. Another amigo introduced me to people with houses for sale. This same fellow was a skilled masseuse and when I was looking stressed spent 25 minutes realigning and massaging my back and neck without charge.

One of the gentlemen my masseuse amigo introduced me to was going to introduce me to an attorney friend of his. I went to his house at the appointed date and time and he invited me into his house and his wife cooked breakfast for the two of us. These experiences were beginning to happen for me here. (Let's give it up for the clean and sober crowd! Hip, Hip, Hooray!)

Nature did abound in every sidewalk crack and wall cranny. I had not taken to the woods but nature was never far away and giant iguanas were living in the trees right across the street from the mall. Small yards were filled with lemon, orange, banana and exotic fruit trees. Beautiful and brightly colored flowers filled the shrubs and trees seemingly at any time of the year. There were more kinds of flowers here than I think I could learn in my lifetime and they were everywhere. You would find them in yards and fields, in parks and plazas, and in unexpected spots in the center of the city.

It was literally perpetual spring here and it was reflected in the farmers market and in the people who lived here. (Did I like it better than in the North? There was no comparison. To each their own.) For me it was all just about love. I just loved something different than those who live in the north.

Admittedly, some things were more expensive here. For whatever reason linens and shoes were priced out of this world. I had always been a discount shopper and the prices here were probably comparable to the standard boutique or high end department store prices up north. True, I was a cheap guy and lived a poor lifestyle and living here could be very inexpensive. I did not pay rent and I think I didn't spend more than $400 a month and that included all my medical costs and buying some furniture.

CHAPTER 16, DAY 52, CHRISTMAS GOOSE

My day 52 was referred to as Boxing Day in some countries. I think this was an arcane tradition of the British gentry giving hand-me-downs to the hired help as there were new items to replace them from Christmas. However, I was writing about Christmas in Costa Rica and just like in the States it mostly revolved around food and friends.

Traditionally, they had tamales and chicken or some pork main dish. I had two tamales from the day Don Jose did a massage for Don Lester and his wife gave them to Jose to have dinner with me that night. Don Jose and I ate soup and bread that night and I froze the tamales for five days so we could have them for Christmas. I craved some northern traditions so I set my mind to work on menu planning.

Christmas Eve day was filled with unaccepted invitations, trips to the store, cooking and Magic Jack calls to friends in the States. There were no croutons, cranberry sauce, eggnog, fruit cake, pumpkin pie, sweet potatoes or other northern traditions. I became a commander of the kitchen and I improvised in ways that brought some of the northern Christmas to the south.

I had no toaster and no croutons, but I did find some thick pretzel sticks that could be broken by hand into little enough chunks and mixed them with a sautéed collection of yellow onion, garlic, celery, green onion, cilantro and diced pepperoni. Mixed with a little of the chicken grease from the pre-cooked chicken that I bought at the store and this was just like the real deal.

The chickens were selling out at the store and I had to go twice and was lucky to purchase the last one from the second batch of the morning. Nothing to do with the chicken except wait till morning and put my homemade stove top stuffing into the cavity and reheat. It wasn't turkey but it was a reasonable substitute for me and in keeping with the local tradition. Both chicken and stuffing turned out fine for me and Don Jose. Well, he seemed to like the chicken. The people here were very fussy eaters and unwilling to try much that was new or different. Possibly they had set their minds against some foods from some prior experience or opinion.

I was also shopping at the farmers market and lucked into an American style hunk of celery. Most celery here looked like the green makings of hemp rope: small, scrawny and stringy. The big stalks were three times the price and worth the money. With pimento stuffed green olives and American style cream cheese from the store I was on my way to the stuffed celery my momma use to make. Salad fixings were easy to pick up and some American style ranch dressing made it all seem familiar.

There were shelves and shelves full of many different kinds of mayonnaise. Salad dressings as I knew them from up north were rare. Also potatoes were not traditional here. They used yucca which was a tougher root that was sliced, boiled and deep fried. I pan fried a little just to have the local equivalent of the potato. Maybe with a masher and garlic yucca might be more to my liking. It was pretty tough and I don't deep fry. Potatoes were available here and I would use them next time.

The *Gringo* bakers from Atenas had apple crumb cake that I had purchased before I saw the raisin white bread that would have been more like the seasonal brioche available up north. The apple cake was nice but not very reminiscent of Christmas past. The Danish butter cookies from the store tasted like Christmas and the eggnog substitute made from yogurt, banana and ice cream was a hit with my guest.

There was a mixed fruit kefir available in the stores here that was whitish in color and I mixed that with a small banana and a couple heaping tablespoons of vanilla ice-cream and let the magic bullet do its job. It was yummy, rich thick and sweet but still not eggnog. The real surprise was a call for electrical help the day after Christmas from a *Gringo* Realtor that proffered a lunch that culminated in pumpkin pie with real pumpkin pie filling. What a treat!

CHAPTER 17, DAY 52, GIRLS

Day 52 was girls, girls, girls. My friend Jerry from Oregon asked for some dirt on the babes. Generally these stories were written for a mixed audience that included family and female friends. Needless to say I did not get into the dating scene in these missives. This was a belated Christmas gift for the guys.

Most crude of all they say the local gals really liked to, how to put it… have sex. I guessed the guys did too. Costa Rica had a reputation as a promiscuous culture and flirtations took many forms. When I was here in 2009 there was this super sexy, super cute, young gal who was on the make for John. John (a hotel neighbor whose patio I had frequented), who had to be in his 60's, was tall and slender and had a full head of hair. It was probably his constant pursuit of every gal that made him so attractive to them.

He put it this way, "girls here really want to be wanted" and he was a shameless flirt. Every girl was a potential conquest and as he was pouring it on the girls were eating it up. Back to the cutie from the year before; she would give me looks and made an effort to remember my name and spoke to me in English. One day I was sitting on the deck talking to her and out of the blue she flips up her pleated plaid schoolgirl skirt to completely reveal her tidy whitey smooth as silk on top her perfectly brown legs. It seemed her boyfriend did not mind and open relationships were common. From the talk, you would think that everybody was sexing everybody.

It was said that the gals _all_ shaved "down there" as part of the locally enhanced sexual awareness I imagine. I had a chance to see for myself when staying at John's rental in San Isidro. I had a busy day: a bus ride to San Jose (four hour round trip) for business; returned to the house to use the phone to make follow-up calls, and; I bussed to Grecia to get some other business done. The San Jose business was not complete and I needed to call back with info and questions but there was a party for three going on in the front room near the phone.

It was about 2:00 PM and John had: his girlfriend; another gal; loud TV music; beers; and lots of cigarette smoke, and I was invited. I would have just liked some quiet for the phone and my trip to Grecia was partly an excuse to stay away from the scene. (Most would say I was not much of a drinker and that I don't like drinking scenes.) I was also in the early stage of a leg infection and not really feeling that well.

When I returned that night the party raged on and John came to me and asked if I wanted to "have" the girlfriend's friend as she was ready and willing. I however, literally sick and tired, would've given my left leg for some peace and quiet. In closing there was no wild sex story to share here. John did end up in a three-way with her and his now ex-girlfriend. These gals can be possessive and even dangerous if you believe the stories.

However, I was now in love. For three weeks I did nothing but rest and go to the *Farmacia* for wound cleaning and dressing changes. I never did mention that the *Doctora* was a beautiful young woman who had half her breast showing above her tight shirt. She was petite, shapely and had a beautiful face and smile. During my first exam she rubbed her arm against my privates and on the last two cleanings was getting my underpants really wet with the sterilized water. I was not responsive and her interest was waning and I was not flirting overtly.

My new *Tico* friend Don Jose had been walking me around town to meet his lady friends. He constantly offered to find me a girlfriend or a one-night stand and I believed he could have. Another local past time was to hook up people. Everyone seemed to want you and their single friends to meet. If you're looking for sex, they wanted to connect you with someone for sex. Even John, who could not share expenses and was not generous in many ways, offered me his ex-girlfriend or to introduce me to some gals who just liked to have sex. (Somehow he seemed to meet many women. Perhaps it was all the beer and drug parties that attracted them to him.)

CHAPTER 18, DAY 57, HAPPY NEW YEAR

Day 57 was New Years Eve Day and what better day to write about drinking alcohol. Drinking is a cross cultural occurrence. Every culture has its own alcoholic beverages, customs and drinking events. Some Nordic country invented the honeymoon: upon a daughter's marriage the father-in-law was obliged to keep the groom sloshed on honey wine for one lunar cycle; after that... the honeymoon was over.

Native Latin cultures have their corn beer and events requiring mass intoxication. In the US. New Years Eve keeps the champagne (or should I say, "sparkling wine") industry alive. (Though, some of us like to support the sparkling apple cider industry during what was referred to as the holiday season.) In any event, drinking booze is accepted and revered around the world. I have done my share of heavy alcohol consumption and will still have a beer or wine and have been known to slam back the Jack every now and again.

However, talking about drunks... (I might have been hit on the head as a kid and my brain circuitry was off because of it. I knew those automatic responses were self-destructive but somehow unavoidable.) The drunks and I knew better and continued in self-destructive patterns due to some cerebral electro-chemical events that were beyond our control. If this never happened to you then you're one of the lucky ones. Chronic drinkers had built neural pathways that brought about certain predictable behavior patterns and boozers fit right in here in Costa Rica. There seemed to be a forgetful and myopic point of view that prevailed here. There were problems with people giving good directions, few people here remembered to keep appointments and if you were not right in front of them, people seemed to forget you existed.

I questioned whether I had fallen into a land full of alkies and I had. Drinking and smoking cigarettes were national pastimes for *Gringos* and *Ticos* alike. The difference between US drunks and Costa Rican drunks was that the Costa Rican drunks were not looking to pick fights; as a group they were passive, happy drunks. However, they tended to be just as inconsiderate, unpredictable, obnoxious, self-centered and sloppy as any drunk in the US It was hard to tell the drinkers from the non-drinkers here in Costa Rica. The nondrinkers here acted like they were chronic drinkers even if they never drank in their lives. I wrote about the direction problems and the passive aggressive behaviors that were akin to the alcoholic mind-set. *Gringo* and *Tico* alkies felt right at home here. Finding nondrinkers here over the age of 18 seemed almost impossible. Finding ex-drinkers had started to happen for me and even their brain chemistry was still crossed up and they maintained much of the faulty thinking that drinkers had.

I only hoped I could dumb down enough to acculturate. That was one aspect of having bad language skills that was to my advantage. I always felt and looked stupid to the locals due to my language and cultural ignorance. The frustration factor acquiesced to my sense of humor. Every day it grew easier to find humor in the local behaviors as time and financial pressures passed, though I had little tolerance for the constant complaining of the hard core drunks.

I too was prone to the occasional complaint session but I just didn't have the requisite skills to find problems with everything all the time. I had a modicum of gratitude in my soul that occasionally saw the good in a situation. Though I heard the occasional "gracias" from a drunk it seemed to lack sincerity. Their despair was so great they could only go through the motions of appreciation. Perhaps it was that downtrodden nature of the *Tico* that constructed a genetic pattern of neural pathways that so resembled the chronic drinkers. The behavior somewhat resembled depression.

Hope you lifted one on New Year's Eve and slammed back all the happiness you could find in the following year. I did not judge you I was merely an observer and reporter with the limited perspective of a human being flawed by my own genetic, familial and cultural shortcomings. HAPPY NEW YEAR!

CHAPTER 19, DAY 58, IT IS SO LOUD

Day 58 was the first day of a new year, and I wrote about screaming. (You know about yelling at the top of your lungs.) As infants, we practiced every time we were hungry, frustrated, wet or soiled. As a child, in northern culture, that habit was trained out but it was not trained out here. Shouting was a time honored tradition here in Costa Rica. This was mountain country and though yodeling never caught on there was a message and warning system in the primitive culture of yelling from ridge to ridge, up the canyons and across the flat lands. Now it was a favorite form of advertising here. TV ads for the lottery, tires and other shows consisted of only 30 to 60 seconds of screaming. (It was easy for the script writers but please hit the mute button.)

Today's *Tico* relied on verbal communication as opposed to the written word. No predawn station wagons were slapping papers on porches. First, they would be stolen and secondly they just were not brought up developing reading skills. I didn't think there was the focus here for the concentration required to read for 15 minutes. This ADDHD behavior stems from the brain circuitry. I understood this because everyone prefers to do the things they excel at. So instead of station wagons with papers in the morning there were cars with big speakers on top in the afternoon. "Buy, buy, and buy" they screamed and this was barely understandable over the roar of the speakers blaring music on the sidewalks from the stores. Loud was everywhere: people shouted to their friends; heavy base popped out of the back of Honda Civic low riders; loud conversation on the corner or in the lobby while you're on the phone and crack heads that moved furniture upstairs above my head at 3:00 in the morning. I needed a home just to have a place to find some quiet.

You either loved or hated the blaring Spanish assaulting your ears as you walked down the city street. (Was it any wonder that most children's play here was punctuated with shrieks and shouts?) You could send a child to fetch a sibling however they would just shout for them at the top of their lungs. They would never consider going to retrieve them. Many Latin adults maintained this habit. One day, I felt the shout of "HEY"…"HEY"…"HEY" directed toward me across the central plaza of the Apartments. I was learning to tune out the unwanted attention seekers in *Tico* fashion. If it was not important to me it was not at all important. (This was partly self centeredness and partly necessary for maintaining sanity here.)

I had found out that my mom died the night before, so I was in no mood to be accosted by some brain injured crack head for a cigarette which I didn't have or a short-term loan that would never be repaid. No moral imperative stopped any *Tico* from; approaching a stranger for money or smokes; shouting in your ear for another who was far away; cranking up the music when you were on the lobby phone; blasting their horns; igniting fireworks close to others or what seems to be the intentional activating of car alarms. (I can't be sure about activating the alarms but they were certainly intentionally not turning off their roaring car alarms.)

(Yea I did say my mom had died and that was weird timing.) Last July when I had an offer coming in on my house in Cottage Grove Oregon, my dad died. Now I was in the middle of a home purchase here and my mom passed away. Well, I expected these things to happen but it was still a bit of a whack to my psyche. I could have used a good scream or something.

Things that were dead here rotted and vanished quickly. This emotional dampener was dried by the warmth of the jungle air. Just like my Christmas experience in this land of make-believe nothing seemed very real here. It never really felt like Christmas even with the presence of the lights, trees and gift wrap. My mom's passing was real yet somehow it did not feel like I thought it should. Costa Rica changed everything from how it should have been to how it was. "*Asi fue*" (so it was) was a common expression here. It was not like there was anything I could do to change what was. There was only the internal experience to deal with. Everything outside was outside. (I was so looking forward to the Hotel owner's New Years Eve party but I decided to pass on it.)

CHAPTER 20, DAY 59, GHOSTS OF FRIENDS

On day 59 I was thinking about my friends both here and abroad. In my lifetime there were numerous occasions when I tried to convince my parents to cash in their LA equity and buy elsewhere. Their three bedroom suburban home was worth a quick half million bucks and they could have replaced it with a mansion elsewhere for half the price and kept the rest tax free. They always said they could not move because they would miss their friends. This was the same reason that many people gave me for not being able relocate from their lives in the States to a life in paradise.

It seems all of my parents closest friends either drifted apart from them or moved. Ironically their closest friends had moved to locations I had already suggested to my folks. (Do you think your friends would not up and move if their lives led them elsewhere? Don't count on it!) Some of you might do well to examine the depth of your friendships and to question the loyalty of those relationships before making life decisions based on your assumptions.

I made no bones about the fact that there were many challenges to relocating. Hopefully by paying attention to my follies you will avoid a few of your own. However, loss of friends was not necessarily one of them. Though I do miss some of the activities we shared I seemed to have as much contact or maybe more through the internet.

Nevertheless I didn't see their faces when they were deceiving me and it slowed down my receipt of their venomous replies to my innocent prater. Heck I received that kind of insincerity and passive aggressive behavior from strangers and passing acquaintances in Costa Rica. I found many more superficial friendships here than I ever did in the US. Most people here were outgoing and friendly and would be happy to tell me anything to make me happy or "keep the good."

On the other hand there were *Gringos* here who were hungry for solid American relationships and *Ticos* who were honest drug-free Christians looking to make American friends. I had more unrequited kindness shown to me in my short stay here than in my entire life up north. It is true that there were rip-offs here. (Don't kid yourself into thinking you aren't being taken advantage of in the US) I watched my friends lie to their other friends and then tell me they would never lie to me. I had my US friends refer to my writing about the death of my mother as "antics" and I have been told that referring to Costa Rica as a land and people touched by God was a personal insult and insinuated that the reader was not spiritual.

People here were more honest even if less direct. I think I preferred being shunned by those who do not like me and being told lies in order to keep things nice. *Ticos* were not embarrassed about that. *Ticos* were more embarrassed by being caught. A *Tico* buddy had a pack of smokes and ripped the cellophane off in his teeth and spit it on the ground. Three days later I mentioned it to him and he kept saying; "You saw me do that? You saw me do that?"

In the US there would have been a cover-up, lie or a rationalization. Here it was, "*Asi es.*" (So it is) and I am embarrassed you saw me. The act was the act and the only consideration was how the two of us would continue along as buddies now that the act discovered. Maybe I would hear a big story about how hard life was for them and how they need my money but rarely did I hear a rationalization of any action.

Often I received email grief for my efforts to share my story with my US friends and family. Little attention seemed to be paid to the details of the stories. There were also those who shared compliments and my continued thanks went out to them.

CHAPTER 21, DAY 81, MAKING A HOME

I sat until the screen went black. Not for lack of thoughts but because of my lack of desire to connect. I was still distraught over all the changes. My mother's death was so final. All l could think of writing was, "poor me, poor me." It was great here but I was here so it must not have been all that good here. Ha ha ha...

This was my third Sunday in the house, and the neighbors were thinking whatever they were thinking. I had made a show of cleaning the front wall cover for two Sundays and met a few of the neighbors. Kids gave me hard looks. I heard profanities on the other side of the wall in adolescent tones. It was assumed that I was a rich *Gringo*, because I came here and bought a house. Actually, I must have been rich just because I was a *Gringo*,

Costa Rica my heart's devotion... I had already crunched my monthly bills at $300 a month plus lodging. I added up the food receipts from December 12 for about two months and my grocery store receipts, including the farmers market, were about eight dollars a day or fifty dollars a week. That money was spent buying anything I wanted including fancy foodstuffs for Christmas and some food wasted to spoilage. I also bought sundry items like cleaning and juicing supplies and some odds and ends. I could have eaten three good meals a day at cafes for as little as eighteen dollars a day.

After two weeks in the house I had not established any routines. I was still moving furniture about. I was waiting for the mothballs to take effect in a cabinet. (I was told this could be effective purgative for a mild mousey smell that cabinets get from lack of regular use.) My shared wall neighbor came to tell me we share a wall or we're best buddies or just that we were in it together; I don't know what he was trying to say because I could not understand his Spanish at all.

(So it was day what? I had to look it up. Day 81! Where did 22 days go?) Just as if I were Stateside I put myself to work on the biggest project and picked up the odds and ends along the way. (What work could a $50,000 house possibly need?) I wanted to take care of a couple rusty roof panels and might as well make it all one color. I decided on a white roof to reflect the sun off of this cozy pink cottage.

There was scraping, anti-corrosion treatment and primer on the rough spots, then primer on the whole roof and then finally three coats of paint that seemed to dry slowly. I had to special order the white paint because it was not a standard color here in Costa Rica. Most common was red followed by green then rust and last there was new galvanized metal. To buy the paint it involved some four hours of bus rides and price changes that would spin your head. In the end I paid the original offered price for the paint delivered to my door and the overpriced extras were returned with the delivery guy.

I decided that replacing some of the screws and replacing all the nails with screws would be intelligent. I started by buying 20 screws and went back for another 20 screws and then back again for 60 more screws. Every time I returned to the hardware store I paid a different price. Even the fourth time, when I went in with an old receipt, the price was different again. I just a dollar here and a dollar there but it all added up. I just abhorred feeling like I was being taken advantage of.

After purchasing the house, it came up short a few possessions: plants; plant stands; phone; mirror; spoons and who knows what little odds and ends had also been taken. The Realtor met to help me understand the utility bill paying details and when I spoke of the missing stuff she became visibly upset and her reply was that she had only received a thousand dollars for her ten hours of work. Then she said she would like to receive another $2,500.00 from me. Her boss said he was going to give her that amount but he did not.

CHAPTER 22, DAY 86, EVERYWHERE I GO

On day 86 I had grown a little confused. It seems I brought all my insecurities, fears, emotions and flawed human characteristics with me. I would have thought that being in this beautiful place would have melted away my old self and I would have been born again to the bliss of the universe. (This is dry east coast sarcastic humor and I knew better than to expect moving to make things better.) Anywhere I went; there I was. If you move to paradise you need to be prepared to meet yourself there.

This was the most beautiful place I had ever spent five hours laying paint down on a hot tin roof in the glaring sun. The roof was taking on an entirely new feel. God willing I will not go back up for repairs for another five to ten years. I had been working three to four hours a day putting on coat after coat of long lasting protection. I was still worried in general. I worried about whether my immigration papers were submitted or not. I worried about finding a taxi ride to San Jose at 4 AM for a last minute trip to Nicaragua?

I was starting to hang some of the curtains that were left behind and fixing some hangers in need of repair. I made a small hanging garden in the breezeway. My household goods were getting organized. I had a small simple kitchen working. I made chicken soup with a smoked chicken. I saw a ring eyed beast that looked like a cross between a squirrel and a mountain lion [wouldn't you know it was called a *gato del monte* (cat of the mountain)]. I was beginning to appreciate that I lived on the edge of a nature preserve and the sightings it would afford. I had begun to take all the bird calls and bird sightings for granted. There were not too many bugs but you did not want to dip a spoon in sugar and leave it sitting on the kitchen counter. The weather was blissful and I had my first flood in the laundry room.

The *Tico* washer was not a US washer. There were some regular washers down here. However, the *Tico* washer was a contraption that used two tubs, three dials and a manually operated drain switch. Manual means that one turns the water on and watches for it to reach the fill level and then turns the water off. Almost self explanatory once I understood about the load size and soap extraction. One tub was for wash and rinse and utilized a fill and drain button. The other tub was for the spin cycle and though it did not dry the clothes, it spun much of the moisture out of them. The indoor clothesline finished most jobs in just one sunny day.

One time I managed to leave the water filling the tub when I started a cycle and came back to discover how overflowing water escaped the laundry room. By sunset I pretty much had the whole load dry. The *Tico* washer was a time consuming labor saving device that required attention every 10 to 15 minutes but it saved me from hand scrubbing. I eventually figured out the soap extraction and the process washed a small load in about an hour.

Everything was protracted here. Things were neither quick nor easy. I often wondered what effect the constant moving of the earth must had on people living in Costa Rica. I usually only noticed it when I was lying on the bed, sitting or leaning against a wall or generally being very still. Sometimes it felt like the earth was moving in small circles and it was sort of massaging or lulling. I never noticed these movements when I was active, moving or paying attention to an activity but they happened frequently. I had heard that you could go to Fortuna and feel the ground rumble constantly and hear the volcanic action "24/7." I had not yet connected the movement of the earth with the "live for today," "be in the moment," "take what you can" mentality that prevailed here but I thought there was one.

CHAPTER 23, DAY 87, I AM PSYCHIC

It was odd that I (who was such a poor traveler and would really prefer to be hanging out around the house) was making this leap. I needed to consider the *Pura Vida* hang loose life style a bit more. I wondered if I would retire into anything. People asked me for my electrical expertise!! Journeyman: Have skills will travel. I was not writing about travel. I was writing about being a stranger in a strange land. This was an expat diatribe not a travel writer's journal.

On day 87 I wrote about all the crazy weird stuff about which you've been waiting to hear. Two sheet sets were left in the house by the seller Donna Inez. One of them almost matched a set I brought with me in color, design and trim. She also left a Pyrex bowl that had a rubber cover. There was an additional rubber cover that fit no other bowls in the house but it fit the Pyrex bowl that I brought with me. Another oddity was the desert forks. Desert forks were those delicate delectable kitchen utensils saved for ceviche, low fondues and any kind of sweet-thing you could eat with a fork. (It gives one pause to linger over the gormandizing event.) Thanks to Jody Huckins I had a pair of said specialty tools and deemed them worthy of the two dollars a pound freight charge so I brought them along.

My dear sainted patroness left four desert forks in the silver drawer for me here at *Casa Rosa* (Pink House). There were just too many of those little things to be merely coincidental. It was downright synchronistic, an affirmation of being in the right place at the right time. I was beside myself from the experience. The numerous and incredible experiences intertwined with the everyday challenges of existing in someone else's paradise. Then, there was the story of the invisible woman:

When I had an interaction with someone I usually said that I had met them. However, I could not say that I had met the invisible woman because she was invisible. It was at the end of a long day during which I had purchased some groceries but no fruit. I decided to stop at a fruit stand I had seen. I was not looking forward to the negotiation for some bananas and avocados. (The more tired I was the worse my Spanish became.) While picking through the avocados I heard a female voice address me. I assumed it had addressed me because the word avocado/*aguacante* was in the sentence. I nodded politely and gave a quick glance in an attempt to discourage a Spanish avalanche of smiling niceties.

I had my selection gathered and was putting the bananas in my bag and was asking *cuanto questa*? (How much cost?) The clerk blurted out something incomprehensible in Spanish and the female voice said to me in perfect English that he needs to count the bananas to give me a price. Still engrossed with the monumental task ahead of me of paying for my goods and finishing my business I heard the voice again. That time she was translating the price with no discernible accent at all. Each time I had nodded, gestured or said thanks and when I was done the body that was attached to the voice was gone.

I saw people all the time. When I walked by people on the street, did some transaction or just nodded and said "*Adio*,'" I was usually left with some feeling about that person. I would usually remember something such as a feature, a color, shape or essence. Maybe I couldn't describe them but I would recognize something about them. This gal, however, was gone. I couldn't tell you anything about her. I would never recognize her if I were to see her again. It was as if she never really existed at all or perhaps I was just losing my marbles.

Everything in Costa Rica was magical. There was enough of everything to be here in the house comfortably. I was sleeping in the guest cot and that sufficed. With the added expense of border adventures and the anxiety it produced in me I decided to wait until I had a better understanding of finances before buying a new bed. Oddly enough a good mattress was inexpensive down here; $150 for a nice matrimonial/double quilted top. A bed frame at $400 as well as other furniture I looked at seemed expensive.

I eventually bought a bed frame and a mattress and had a mosquito net from Real Goods? I was going to try my new bed in the master bedroom for the first time.

I couldn't sleep there! I did not know why but the room, bed, mattress, sheets or something in there was giving me insomnia. I could go back to the guest room and I would sleep fine there but the master bedroom kept me restless and I even ended up waking in the middle of the night.

I eventually went back to sleeping on the guestroom cot after an invasion of flies entered the master bedroom. There must have been a total of 50 flies. All the flies were easily killed one at a time as they seemed attracted to clinging to the mosquito net. Since then, I tried the room again only to wake again in the night. Someone suggested I sleep in the guest room and rearranging the furniture was in my future.

CHAPTER 24, DAY 93, GRANADA, NICARAGUA

After an 11 hour bus ride Moorish colonial architecture awaited me in Granada. The gem of Nicaragua, its oldest city, was reported to be a must see. I must see it because I had not received my immigration application yet! Even with the receipt of my papers in process the ARCR told me I still needed to cross the border every 90 days until the application was complete and I had an accepted applicant status.

Before applying they said once they received an email confirmation of the application no more border runs were required. I guess this will be the first of many trips. Maybe I will discover how to make it a cheap shopping trip to Miami or do more sightseeing in Nicaragua or Panama. In April, I would be back in Oregon with an opportunity to see my friends and I was so looking forward to that trip.

It was day 93 and you might have wondered why I went to Nicaragua. Vacation? R & R? Much needed rehab from what seemed like endless painting on the roof? It was necessary to renew my visa by leaving the country every 90 days. This was the way many *Gringos* stayed long-term in Costa Rica. They made what was called a "border run" every three months and renewed their passport visa which was usually good for an additional 90 days.

Some clever folks had their passports renewed at the border without actually going out of the country. Some ignored this procedure entirely and just stayed in-country and never crossed the border and therefore their passport was not checked and their visa was not renewed. If they did attempt to fly out of the country there might be fees to pay and worst of all they could be asked not to come back to the country for a year or more.

The people at ARCR had said that once I filed I would not have to do border runs. Once all the documents were in place and they had my money it was an entirely different story. Then, I had to do border runs for the next nine months or year. Sometimes Latin thinking really bothered me. The whole loosey goosey thing was new to me and I just couldn't take it personally.

In Nicaragua I bought a milkshake. The menu said 30 Cordovas, tax was not included. The tax rate in Nicaragua was 15% and the bill came to 37.90 Cordovas because it included the tax and a 10% gratuity. So, the dollar fifty shake really sold for two dollars and a ten dollar dinner was really twelve fifty, mind you it was a great dinner. In Costa Rica the "*impuesto*" (tax) was often used as a way of raising the price in an indisputable way. Sometimes taxes only apply it to *Gringos* or people of wealth.

As a way of life I found these border trips expensive, disruptive and tedious. This was probably why so many *Gringos* just stop renewing their visa. The beginner in me took the safe routes: Taxi transportation to the Express bus; hotel reservations; advance transportation tickets; carry-on luggage only; prearranged assistance with customs and a clean change of clothes for each day. It cost less than $300 for the 4 days including transportation, food and lodging.

It was worth every penny to go to a historic place (read - turn of the century) that felt like a trip to the U.S: Steak and baby back ribs; Nicaraguans speaking perfect English to each other over lunch; US style spa and hotel accommodations with helpful and enthusiastic counter staff. The nearly fluent English of the hotel staff garnered my confidence of an easier journey. The hotel price was very good considering all the amenities: fluffy towels, pool towels, hot water in the shower and tap, full breakfast, purified water, strong wifi, a/c (and you wanted air conditioning and/or at least a fan) and a flat screen TV with 100 cable channels.

Granada itself was a Knott's Berry Farm type of deal. The facades looked like some old timey buildings from the turn of the century and the people were pretending to be someone they were not. They were characters out of Hemmingway novels of quaint old time carriage drivers who now just drove from the front of the park to the front of the park. Granada was a place of photo opportunity or artistic inspiration and not a camera or a pallet was to be seen.

Tourists used Granada as a recreational base camp and went out of town on adventures returning to their American style food and lodging. Very few *Gringos* were on walkabouts yet *Gringos* filled the hotels, restaurants and bars. I guessed I just didn't understand what it meant to act like a tourist. Granada had that <u>West World</u> feeling of being safe, where "nothing can go wrong" combined with the sense that there was danger lurking somewhere nearby.

There were armed guards outside the banks as there were in Costa Rica. However, I only saw a couple of cops in the whole town. I did not feel like I wanted to go into the Bizarre alone. There were plenty of very "White" that felt safer. The crowded stalls and dingy back streets with people bumping into each other did not appeal to my sense of safety. If I were robbed or detained trying to find a cop would not be easy.

The tourists' services in the heart of town were mostly hotels, bar eateries, art galleries, chocolate filled menus, gift shops, tour offices, boutiques and gorgeous buildings. The architecture might have been turn of the century Spanish Adobe but the food selections felt like downtown USA. There were steak houses, Mexican restaurants, Italian kitchens and pizzerias, Chinese, a waffle house, chic salad cafes and a plethora of breakfast/lunch places. Except for the one food cart I noticed, the fare was not typically Nicaraguan.

The buildings included: many churches, schools, a convent, a hospital, the Red Cross, large offices and homes. Many were just homes and some were just fronts with construction projects behind the doors. The poorer parts of town that I walked into were of the same flavor as the colonial homes in color and layout just much smaller and run down and of inferior materials. There were both good and bad parts of town in the non-historic areas. An English speaking taxi driver on a two hour jaunt around the area could reveal the other parts of the city. Though the taxis drove so fast you might not notice much.

This was a happening town with dancing and live music bars. I think visits early in the week would be the quietist but Friday and Saturday night's rock. One hotel manager told me, "You were either joining the party in the bar and restaurant on Saturday night or you would not be happy here." Many restaurants were attached to hotels and many bars were attached to restaurants. There was also a sizable group of coffee bars with only breakfast fare.

I never saw a grocery store or even a fair sized *pulperia* (corner market). I barely remember seeing a couple of small seedy looking *sodas* (small lunch counters). So, you either bring food, feed the tourist food machine in Granada or find a market. There could be food in the Bazaar but I never went in the area to see. Later I discovered there was a large market just outside the historic district.

I brought Peanut butter, bread, carrots, apples, cookies, water and mixed drinks in pop bottles to keep me sleeping on the bus. The drinks worked and the rest fed me both ways and made some snacks at the hotel. Breakfast was part of my package so I ate a big breakfast and snacked for lunch and ate out for dinner.

I bet I could have the same trip for half the cost now. I would love to go back and just wander around the streets taking more photos. Women and men still carried baskets on their heads and the horse carts and architecture really captured my attention. I looked forward to going back some day and staying more modestly. Perhaps I could find some humble eateries and exploring outside the tourist zone. (Renting bikes might be fun but it is hot.)

The only better trip would have been a stateside trip to Home Depot, Harbor Freight and Ross with empty suitcases and a credit card. Perhaps July, when my next 90 days comes due I might enjoy the breeze off of Lake Nicaragua. Some unpleasant aspects about that town was its' clicks, snobs, and the fact that I looked like one of the local characters so my reputation preceded me without my earning it.

CHAPTER 25, DAY 97, QUARTERLY REVIEW

On day 97 I wrote a quarterly review. (Luckily for you your life was probably more of the same old, same old.) I thrust myself into a new country, culture and community where it was all was new and different and I had a few thoughts. I was still not cynical, just wary.

Costa Rica was hard on possessions. From washing machines that wear the rim off your cap to waiting in long lines that wear the rim off your patience. Everything you bring will eventually break, be broken by the environment or be mishandled by the untrained locals. Ha ha ha... Of the things I brought two kitchen items had been broken since I arrived and they were not broken by me. It was beautiful here and the weather was spectacular. But like my daddy used to say, "If you want to feel secure in your relationship marry a plain woman not a pretty one."

I'm not talking about spending a few weeks in a resort filled with so much awe that you couldn't tell what the locals were like. You might have had a good feeling from the hotel clerk and the waiter in the restaurant. You might have found the taxi driver nice and helpful as you peeled off foreign bills that felt like play money. It was only a little overpayment here and a little there and you budgeted for it anyway. However you can't live that way day to day. Daily living means you have to watch your money and the people around you as well.

Often poor people resent rich people. The resort type experience was great because you were just there to spend money and leave. You were not seen as an invader or consumer of their precious resources. I heard the vibe could be quite hostile in parts of Hawaii and the news was full of dreadful reports of kidnappings and robberies in Mexico. Here in Costa Rica things were a little less overt and the culture prevents making accusations.

There were helpful people who appeared to be looking out for my best interest. Even they needed to receive the test of time. Did I need all the stuff the helpful pharmacist suggested or was he just looking for something else to sell me? That questionable filling I received from a dentist was very little money to ruin the enamel on a perfectly good tooth. I was learning to trust no one but myself! I was developing an especially keen sense and I trusted my gut more than ever.

Everything was slow here. I had to take it all in stride. The dentist had kept me waiting 45 minutes as his first appointment for the day. It took a month to get title to the property after the deal was closed. I bring a book to read when I go to the bank. Thanks to some kind of spiritual intervention I did not lose my life's savings in the house deal.

You can make friends with people here but it takes a considerable amount of effort and people savvy. The *Tico* friend who joined me for Christmas and shared time in the park with me and helped me look for houses and worked for me painting the roof ended up stealing about four dollars in cash. It was not about the four dollars. It was that I could no longer trust him to be in the house alone to use the bathroom when we were working on the roof together.

The same larcenies happened in the States it was just a little less rampant because there were a few more recourses. There were no rules here and laws were not enforced and eating the perceived rich was a common practice. I would write about the birds and the sunshine and the trash can made from the paint thinner gallon another time. It was easy to take the spectacle of nature for granted and become overwhelmed by the process of living. I liked to live poor and I felt like I fit in here better than I did up north. Actually most of the local people lived more opulently than I did. As a rule, Costa Ricans rarely walked anywhere or ate at home and most of them spent every dime in their pocket and did not have savings accounts.

Let's look at the money situation again. It was $200 a month for store bought food and if I had rent, it was $300 or more, but then there was eating out, travel, medical costs, air fare, and car rental bills. Let's not forget attorney fees, home repairs and taxi rides along with a high end visa renewal trip to an enchanted city. During my initial transition it appeared I was spending around a $1,000.00 a month. That was transition money and the normal living costs should be much lower once I stop paying rent and flying back and forth to Oregon. It might be cheaper to live in other countries but there were many considerations and tradeoffs. Costa Rica was *muy tranquilo* (very peaceful) and more beautiful than many other countries.

Let's talk banking. Being an expatriate takes money and how much depends on you. I had been fortunate to have a bank with reasonable ATM fees and I paid only two dollars to withdraw funds. Some banks charged as much as $16 to use the ATM. This becomes expensive if you can only withdraw $250 during each transaction. I had my bank raise my limit to $600. Sometimes, I could withdraw only $500, because of the dispensing bank's ATM and that seemed completely random. My credit card was set up on an auto-pay from a checking account and I only had to be sure to maintain an appropriate balance. These conditions needed to be set up with the bank in person before leaving the home country.

The complicated part would be my IRA accounts and social security funds. Let's not even think about the social security application process or cashing out an IRA. I had a 5 year pension coming from a deposit in the *Banco National* but that was my own money and it rolled into a *Colones* (local currency) account. My *Colones* account paid my Costa Rican utilities on auto-pay. I used the *Colones* account as living money and consolidated my accounts in the States. I still worried about the Rentista application which was in process.

I still needed to buy an airline ticket to travel from Oregon to Costa Rica after fling back to Oregon. One solution was to buy a fully refundable ticket and cash in the return flight and another solution was to buy a one-way fare.

For a visa renewal trip I might book a roundtrip ticket to Miami to shop for household and hardware needs. One challenge while using the hardware stores in Grecia was that customarily everything was behind a counter. I had to describe what I wanted in Spanish and hoped they carried the item. Usually someone either ignored me or acted like they did not understand or trotted off to grab what they thought I was talking about and came back with a reasonable facsimile. There was no "shopping" for just the right hardware solution. That was difficult for me because I was a visual person when it came to seeking solutions to mechanical problems.

It was more costly to live in Costa Rica and it was more American than Nicaragua in some ways. I wondered how the *Gringos* in Nicaragua ignored the poverty and squalor directly outside of their small domains. People were generally better off here in Costa Rica than in Nicaragua, but the Costa Ricans thought they had it really bad like their Nicaraguan brothers. It was not just me who could miss the beauty of the moment and revel in the disappointment of unfulfilled dreams. (I guess everybody wanted something and some people just dealt with disappointment better than others.)

Next time I would try a visit to Panama. Poor people or rich people, it was easy to find woe and despair. People here in Costa Rica were probably happier than most people in the world. They have never wanted for food and have never really been enslaved, not even by the quest for basic needs. You might even call Costa Rica a socialist country in some respects. That was all changing but to some degree the customs of sociability and politeness still prevailed.

CHAPTER 26, DAY 103, VALENTINE'S DAY

(Day 103 should have been some kind of landmark.) It was another 6:30 AM warm and sunny morning spent watching the *palomas* (birds) and listening to them mix and match their songs of love. I so enjoyed my coffee on the windowsill watching and listening to the jungle just past my reach. That was the first day that I felt like I had nothing to do. Lord knows there were loads of hobbies to grab my attention: I could study Spanish; I could weed; fix the low edge of the gutter; seek out legal council to push the river on getting my corporation and title papers finished; walk around town and work on my map project; design some business cards; seek legal council to deal with my parent's trust that my brother was not executing; clean some more, or; keep clearing away the garbage heap. Did I mention the garbage heap?

There were any good things in the heap and it was a little like Christmas but with dirt. I had unearthed some climbing vines, a few plant baskets, broken cinder blocks, floor tiles that matched the ones in the house and rocks and bits of plastics. Best of all I found an earthworm amongst the loamy black earth. That dirt compacted upon wetting and was home to the roots of who knows what. It appeared this was a graveyard to more than just Donna Inez's, the seller's, dead and dying plants. The leaves from the lime-like fruit tree, called *Cass*, made wonderful compost for planting and enriching the more depleted areas. The sun and the heavy rains took their toll on the exposed.

I could skip off to paradise without my friends but I was glad I brought my hobbies. I would flounder without some interests that were accessible. I was in the land of the lost where it could be impossible to find any specific item (due to lack of local usage) or it could be prohibitively expensive.

Yard work was the manna of the homebody and until it started raining the yard was fair game for pulling weeds, plant training and trash mound reduction. This was the dry season and the deciduous trees had shed their leaves and plants could be pushed into flowering by watering heavily. The shade plants really wanted their shade and potted plants seemed to need attention.

Cleaning was another homebody past time that had earned the time honored title of virtue. After my day with a hired maid I finished removing the wax build up where the floor tiles met the wall. What a sweet valentine, today I had a cute happy thirty something doing my dirty work for me, as well as walking with me to the store, reading the Spanish packages and making recommendations. After cleaning we had a little *Arroz con pollo* that I had made up the day before. The dish was something that was on its way to becoming chicken soup but it never made it that far.

Having female company was such a pleasant change from interacting with a bunch of guys. It was a common theme...*Gringo* guys, guys, guys were here in Costa Rica and many of them were looking for girls. There seemed to be many girls here they were just not expats. There were some *Gringas* out there; I just had not crossed paths with any of whom I wanted an association. Most of the English speakers I ran into were guys. It was difficult to run into English speaking women. A Spanish speaking woman who I paid a dollar eighty an hour to hang out with, be friendly and help me do my chores was a treat for Valentine's Day. There is nothing like a clean house with a bit of a woman's touch.

It took 100 days to feel like I did not have to do anything right away. There was food in the fridge, LP gas in the tank, electricity and phone bills paid, enough tools and supplies to do some things around the house and enough money to spend on some traveling. (Ha ha ha. Mapping the city center would be more my idea of a great adventure.)

CHAPTER 27, DAY 105, FOREIGN CULTURE

On day 105 it felt like expatriating was all about letting go. It was mostly about letting go on a conceptual basis. I could keep my stuff, I could keep my friends, I could buy new stuff and I could make new friends. However, nothing was really the same anymore. By expatriating I had gained a new perspective on life that was not unique to Latin countries. It was about having left my home country. It did not matter where I went to live or from where I had departed, different was different.

For a few months it felt like a vacation and I was overwhelmed by the uniqueness of the experience and how different the people, things and interactions were. If you were like me you had a strong agenda with a list of tasks you wanted to accomplish. Even if your plan was to sight-see, lie on the beach or watch birds... it was the "other" to which one was attending. (I probably had more than the usual amount of introspective moments because I was infirmed for three weeks.)

No matter what happened with my money, my Rentista application, my business and my stuff in the US I lived here and I had moved into a nice little home to prove it. [You could be renting an apartment in a town, renting a small house in the *campo* (countryside) or traveling around the country, at some point you have to see yourself as living here. Even if you plan to live both "here" and "there," at some point you are no longer a tourist.] The visa renewal run to the border was harbinger of having moved here because when I was returning to Costa Rica I felt like I was going home.

I felt relief on some vague conceptual level and that was so compelling. Nothing was the same anymore and I felt like I was beginning to look at life a differently. I never understood prostitution or buying another person's company until I hired a gal to come clean my house.

Suddenly I could see how one might pay for female companionship. I still had no interest in buying sex; I just had an understanding of why many men do that down here. Until recently I had placed a stigma on that kind of activity and I judged both parties negatively. Somehow my judgmental thoughts had been changed. Maybe it was because so many interactions that I would have judged as negative turned out to be the "norm" here and I could no longer be caught up in what was right and what was wrong. There was also that Zen concept of "*Asi es*" (So it is) that was so prevalent here.

Ignoring the Jiff peanut butter and the Smucker's low sugar strawberry jam that I bought regularly everything was foreign and that made it easier to embrace concepts that were once beyond comprehension. All the weird interactions, unexpected delays and strange reactions brought me to a level of acceptance to which I had not previously evolved. I was still a control freak by some standard and still looked for routine and familiarity to center my life around. But I had gained a newfound ease with the unusual, the unexpected and the unplanned.

Almost everything had an unusual twist to it and almost nothing went as I had expected it to go. However, everything seemed to have some strange serendipity to it that led to the perfect outcome. In my western mind what might have looked to be a challenge, stumbling block or unacceptable outcome often turned out to be... OK. All the little irregularities seemed to just be great opportunities to release preconceived concepts of how life should be. I found myself changing in ways that accepted and interacted with the cultural norm in a way that was best for all.

Don't ask me how the machine kept running; I had not come to understand that. For now my job was to attend to the "me" part of it all. God would take care of the rest.

CHAPTER 28, DAY 107, LONELINESS

On day 107 I experienced my first real hit of loneliness. Probably it was because I had seen the movie "Julia," and watching it I put myself in those relationships which were so full of love. I was moved by my desire to connect with a partner in those ways. However, I could no longer see that in my future. Without the common bond of culture and language the full depth of love seen in the movie seemed very unlikely.

(What's that got to do with your expatriate experience? Just this: bring lots of love with you.) Bring love for yourself. Bring love for strangers. Bring love for the unknown. Most of all bring someone you love with all your heart and who loves you equally. (How did Paul Childs put it in the movie? "The butter for my bread, the breath of my life?")

(OK "Julia" was only a movie. Real life was not a movie: no retakes; no practicing lines; no scripted outcomes; no edited film, it was just action. Yea, I am OK and everything's going to be alright. Sometimes I caught glimpses of the American Dream and I wished I had been able to make them real for me. It didn't happen for me in the US and that was a large part of my deserting the fantasy. Look at Tiger Woods: there was nothing all that perfect about realizing the American dream for him.)

Yea, we all die alone. Monks and nuns live complete and peaceful lives. Everyone leaves everyone in one way or another. Until that time of "until death do you part" you would really appreciate a partner in the transition from where you are leaving to where you are going if expatriation is in your future.

I came to Costa Rica out of a draw to be here but what did I know? I believed the dribble I read in the tour books written by fly-by researchers. In hind sight I read some of those comments more closely and I saw phrases like: "Their brochure says..." and "They told us..." If I sent you the brochure from the Healthy Days Apt and Hotel with the exaggerations highlighted it would be heavily marked.

Everybody had the best of intentions, even if their intentions were to secure your business. Friends trying to recruit your visit or wanting you to move to paradise to be with them also had good intentions. The question of the day was, "How well did I deal with disappointment?"

I guessed that loneliness was part of the reason I wrote. Perhaps it was not the reason I wrote but it was the reason I sent my writing out to others. Similar to my need to not feel stupid, I needed to feel connected. Yes, it was all an illusion. However, those feelings seemed as real as the wood I had purchased the day before to make some home improvements.

The big difference was that I could not measure those feelings, cut them to fit my needs, replace them with something else I desired or go shopping for some different feelings with money alone. When it came to feelings all the greats would tell you there were only Love, Fear, and Detached Attachment. All the subsets of these three were what we experienced.

Having no expectations meant having no disappointments. My advice: be a good boy scout and be prepared. I brought soap and a towel the first time I stayed in a Costa Rican hotel. The clerk told me it was a good thing I hadn't any expectations because many people came here with expectations and were disappointed.

CHAPTER 29, DAY 108, HOBBIES

On day 108 I felt like I was a writer. That speaks to the hobby part of retirement. As a stranger in a strange land I needed to keep myself active. There were shopping, cooking, eating and cleaning up to do. All those were very necessary but not completely satisfying.

I wrote. I wrote about what happened. I wrote about what I thought about what happened. I even went so far as to write about what I thought about what I thought about. In all honesty it was all somewhat illusionary and vague. I have reported facts, given opinions and shared feelings, but would never mean anything significant. Each individual page was just a fleeting moment.

There was no agenda in writing for me. I was here! (Well, I guessed my agenda would have been to create an avenue for internal exploration.) I wouldn't have dared share these conversations with the people who I met every day. I might tell my nine closest friends or even countless faceless strangers who were exploring options in their lives.

I wrote. Some guys entertained. Some guys drank. Some guys chased girls. Some guys watched T.V. Some guys were out to make a few bucks all the time. Not too many gym rats here, but there was a strong café contingency. I had read that in most Latin cities you could find clutches of *Gringos* gathering in various cafes or restaurants.

It was a funny scene to me. It looked like a bunch of stray cats warily eyeing and mewing to each other. There were more *Gringos* in this country that knew everything than you could shake your cocoa powder at. Why bother hanging out with those people who think they know everything when you were the only one who really knew EVERYTHING. The "everything" I knew was, that I knew nothing.

The expatriate experience was an individual quest, and everyone I met dealt with it differently. There were common experiences and some universally recognized aspects of *Tico* culture. Much of what I hypothesized about Costa Ricans had been supported. I found that many of my individual frustrations and longings were shared by others as well.

Some of the facts and feelings I shared might sound or seem untenable but they were just part of the great transition. This book's focus was, "What did Peter not prepare for, and what could you do to make a transition easier for you?"

Sometimes my experiences were real gritty, so don't be discouraged by my difficulties. I transcended them with the help of my stateside friends who remembered me in their thoughts and emails and who I occasionally chatted with on the telephone. It was like the new friend silver and old friend gold saying. After a year passed I had a bigger, brighter and clearer picture of Costa Rica. I only had to remember to take one breath at a time, and repeat as needed.

That did not mean my experiences would be your experiences, nor did it mean that it was a problem. Even the most trying of experiences turned out OK. How did that expression go: My worst day of fishing was better than my best day of working? For all the effort and the angst, Costa Rica was where I had chosen to be.

CHAPTER 30, DAY 109, FOOD

On day 109 it was time to confess that writing had never been a hobby of mine before moving to Costa Rica. However, cooking was a serious pastime I engaged in regularly. Partly it was just to eat because without food the whole machine did not work but mostly it was because I found a great creative opportunity every time I stepped into the kitchen. I really liked eating my work because it was instant gratification!

The first book I was going to write was a cookbook. I was planning a book on how to be creative in the kitchen. Anybody could follow instructions and go and buy the required ingredients and then put them together in the prescribed fashion. My book would have been about how to discover and create recipes. Even Julia learned her receipts from school and her co-authors but someone created all those dishes by some cosmic accident or process of successive approximation.

It could just as well have been you who discovered the three nut-butter sandwich, risotto primavera or faux eggnog. However, I was not here to pitch another book, I wanted to share my food buying and eating habits here in Costa Rica. I may have bought the same groceries all the time but I never prepared them the same way twice.

I bought pretty standard fare that was reasonably priced. My food budget was around $43 bucks a week and I still had to throw some food away. Every day I enjoyed an avocado/cream cheese dip of some kind with chips, fresh squeezed orange juice and a banana/peanut butter/yogurt shake of some kind. I had also found some good multigrain bread in the store and had toast and jam with coffee in the morning followed by some kind of egg dish. Often, I would just grab a boiled egg if I didn't plan on making an egg salad sandwich. He he he

The eggs were magic here. I bought the farm fresh eggs in the plastic bags and not the factory eggs in the crates. They separated beautifully and just boiled or fried they were a thicker consistency and more flavorful than US eggs. For a long time I only saw brown eggs for sale here.

I was able to make the most elaborate salads from the freshest veggies purchased at farmers market. I had found that having favorite vendors paid off. I was now a favored customer at a couple stalls and the avocado guy and the hydroponic lettuce guy threw in a freebie in return for my weekly loyalty.

All the fresh vegetables seemed to last a long time in the fridge. The cheese had a tendency to go sour in a week and sometimes I would skip buying a few veggies if I had leftovers from the week before. The broccoli just did not last here and I had to shop hard to find nice broccoli in the market. But the green beans, green onions, carrots, onion, garlic, cilantro and lettuce all seemed to store well.

I still had no oven so tuna, eggs, cheese and precooked chicken were my main protein sources. I was continuing to make variations of my famous chicken soup. I usually made one pot of soup a week and I ate out of that soup pot until it turns into stew. (Anyone care for a grilled cheese and chef salad? Maria cookies with peanut butter or a yogurt drink? I was not becoming skinny here even though I walked frequently.)

I think the warm weather had curbed my appetite a little. Unfortunately I had made friends with a cooking fool who loved to bake cakes and feed his guests cakes, lunches and sugary fruit drinks. The Colombian *Panaderia* (bakery) had some shortbread-like cookies that I really liked. I bought the cookies two at a time.

CHAPTER 31, DAY 115, TRAVELER'S SICKNESS

On day 115 I had planned to write about words: Spanish words, English words, English words that came from Spanish words and Costa Rican words. At the keyboard I just wanted to be wanted. The word topic was very interesting but I just did not have the energy for it.

It seemed I had contracted a case of Giardia on my trip to Nicaragua and three weeks later it was in full bloom. Last night I was screaming at the tidy bowl a few times followed by a night full of intestinal cramping. Something new for us guys. After that I shared a greater empathy for those women cursed with the affliction. I kept wondering if it was appendicitis and was I going to die in my sleep. Then I wondered who would find the body.

(I didn't know what to suggest to my American contacts if they didn't hear from me for two or three weeks. That was a detail that would be worked out. That was something that was difficult to determine.) Well, I did not die in my sleep. I did extensive research online about my symptoms and I must have contracted the bug from the one time I brushed my teeth in the tap water or from something I picked up in a restaurant. It seemed that some symptoms started right after my return from Granada.

Alba, a gal who spoke some English and was friendly to me, suggested it was stress. She had seen me frequently carrying painting and building materials home and had suggested I was suffering from the stress of working too much. She said that too much work was bad for a person and could make them sick. Another popular Costa Rican belief was that too much reading was detrimental to the brain and made a person crazy. If you considered questioning the established cultural norm crazy then reading would lead to insanity.

I was stressed but not from too much work. I have never worked too much or too hard in my entire life. (That is why I became an electrician; so I could charge outrageous amounts of money for my time and work less.) I was a surf bum at heart and never worked too hard at anything but I was suffering from some emotional stressors.

The immigration process had me totally freaked. There was no confirmation, no inkling of it being processed or even that my file existed. On March first immigration requirements changed and I could no longer afford to become a Costa Rican resident. The scary part was that I purchased a $50k house. I had heard that Costa Rica might not let me back in the country on a 90 day visa at some point.

Somewhere around day 103 or 104 I woke in the middle of the night unable to sleep. I went to the computer to write. The document that I started writing at 2AM was eaten by a 3AM Windows update. I was writing a heartfelt and poetically scripted tome on Costa Rican women. It seemed that it was not meant for your eyes and would remain forever an exercise of the fingers and of the mind.

I had to readdress the topic of the dangers of Costa Rican women again someday. You guys laugh if you will. I always did when other old timers warned me in vague terms to be careful. There was no way to describe the Costa Rican experience. Something mystical or at least unworldly was going on here. Costa Rican gals had some strange powers.

I wrote about the furnishings that were left in the house, the invisible woman and the need to pay attention to intuition like my life depended on it. Trouble only seemed to come when I ignored my gut feelings and thought my way beyond what I knew to be true. Up north I swam against the river and still made headway. Here it seemed I would drown trying.

Well, I had been sick and should have just shut my trap. I was no good at anything when I didn't feel well. My fears and concerns were amplified by my illness.

CHAPTER 32, DAY 118, SPARE CHANGE

On day 118 it seemed like change was what it was all about. There were all kinds of change. I could change my clothes. I could change my mind. I could change my money. I could be given change. I could pray for change. Change could come upon me unexpectedly. The weather changed and so did my friends. In physics, change was considered a constant. Moving was about change. Relocating was about permanent change. Some believe that form precedes essence and physical change could change the way one thinks. Neuro Linguistic Programming is based on that premise of change.

I had changed and was continuing to change. I changed my living situation because I changed my mind about where to live. Here in Costa Rica I was changing faster and more profoundly than I ever expected that I could. It might seem egocentric but I guessed I would continue to change.

I constantly needed to remind myself to stay in the moment and be prepared for change or for the unexpected. The unexpected was another expatriate experience worthy of consideration. Selections in the grocery store seemed to vary daily. Plants bloomed year round and dead things rotted or were eaten rapidly and that all represented change. If you liked consistency you could find that was here too. But change was ever present in the background. The sun did rise in the east every morning and at almost the same time each day.

A *Tico* might greet me and invite me to visit their farm one day, and pretend they did not notice me next to them the following day. Someone who was happy to see me every time we met could turn cold and indifferent in an instant. Were they done obtaining what they wanted from me or did I do something to which they took umbrage? All I knew was they were gone and without explanation or any attempt at resolution.

I didn't want to find myself hanging on to some emotional state that I had created in my head only to watch it disappear into thin air. The locals knew that too and that was why they liked to keep their relationships superficial. They used greetings like *Adios* and say *Que Tal* not expecting me to tell them "what was up?" It was probably also part of the promiscuous nature of the culture. They had many phrases and customs here that helped them not become too attached to others.

Having expectations here was like walking on quicksand. I couldn't expect people to do what they said or be where they said they would be on time or charge the same price each day or charge the price they offered to sell something. In the States I would have taken offence; here I just thought it was funny (it was just helping me to release the inklings of expectation I brought with me). But it wasn't funny anymore; it just was the way it was. I became much more accepting than I ever thought I could be. However, this was not an intentional or conscious change on my part.

Some of my changes were even noticed by my stateside friends. Little rip offs did not bother me nearly as much as they had Stateside. I no longer cared to understand why I was being shunned by someone. I was no longer interested in trying to fix relationship issues. I still had great expectancy but my expectations had been greatly reduced. Attempted grand deceptions that could have ruined me did not throw me into a tizzy.

Possibly, my reduced expectations were the result of increased intuitiveness. I was just no longer surprised when someone scammed me or was only my friend due to selfish motives. I could now see it coming. I could try to fool myself that it was not what it was. I would then become twisted up behind my self-deception but that could happen only because I didn't trust the truth in the first place.

If thoughts were things then the words were something bigger. Maybe it was all the polite talk that was changing me. "In the beginning there was only the word." Maybe it was the words that were the beginning of all change as well as the beginning of all existence. *Asi fue*, so it was. *Asi es*, so it is.

CHAPTER 33, DAY 119, *TICO* SPANISH

On day 119 I really wanted to write about Costa Rican words. There seemed to be as many dialects here as there were microclimates. I didn't travel much so I didn't see the various weather patterns. But I only had to walk down the street of my barrio to hear more variations of Spanish than I could understand.

There was the singing accent, the Indio influence, the slurrrr, theruntogether, and the syllble drop that I was beginning to recognize. There was slang here and what I liked to call Costa Rican. Costa Rican was a group of Spanish words that had different meanings than those of Latin American countries. Same word might mean something different elsewhere or be a word unique to Costa Rica. It was always frustrating spend a tremendous amount of energy memorizing a Castilian Spanish word only to have a local tell me they used a different word for that here.

Luckily the locals (even with their different words) understood much of my Mexican Spanish. I cannot begin to assist you in understanding all the variations as I was just learning them myself. I wanted to address the words and phrases most commonly used that I believed were affecting how I thought and felt. As an acculturating expat those words had an effect upon me. However, as a tourist none of that would matter. Any Ugly American could avoid being influenced by the hand of God scooping them up and delivering them to paradise.

I was being influenced by the constant usage of many phrases. The word I used most was *Adios*. It was used to greet my neighbors as I walked past them and was often sung out in reply. It was used also when passing complete strangers on the street. We shouted it back and forth when a friend drove by in a car or on a *moto* (motorcycle). It was even used when eye contact was made with a store clerk as I walked down the sidewalk. Here in Costa Rica it meant hello more than it meant goodbye. You might translate it to "hey."

There was also *Buenos dias* (Good days) and *Buenas tardes* (Good afternoon) that were used interchangeably with *Adios*. Most often shortened to *Buenos* or *Buenas,* and all five expressions would vary by the time of day and the perceived relationship with the other person. That sounded arbitrary and subtle and it was. To thicken the stew I added *Senor/Senora* or used *Senor* only depending on the amount of respect due to the other person. They liked to add *Amigo* in their salute to me but I was not yet that presumptuous.

The next most commonly used expression was *Con permiso?* (With permission?). I used it whenever I entered a building. People expected me to stop and ask it before entering their home. It would be followed by an invitation of *Pase adelante* (pass forward) to enter the home or office. Store clerks would reply in stride when I used it as I entered a store. It might even be accompanied by a hand shake and *Buenos Dias* if there was a male clerk by the door. It was "With your permission" and "If I May" and "Excuse me." *Could I* and *I want* were not that commonly used even to the waitress, it was *Con permiso* or *me gustaria* (I would like). I just think humble. I had set *Con permiso* on auto pilot so as to not forget it when it mattered.

Of course, there was the ever-present *Gracias* and *Con mucho gusto* and any chance to be gracious here was utilized. This was a land of genteel language. Standards might be set lower for *Gringos* but any act of gratitude was well received. There was plenty to be grateful for here and I would hear others say *Gracias* often.

Unlike Mexico the reply *De nada* (Of nothing) was not often used. One did not dismiss *Gracias* with "It was nothing" rather it was *Con mucho gusto*, (With much pleasure.) that you received the others thanks. Though you will see it in my writing I did not have much opportunity to use *Asi es* and *Pura vida* in speaking. These phrases influenced me as there was an "it was as it was" and "wasn't it just grand" outlook on life here. I hear them more than I use them but I think these words were a profound influence on everyone here.

CHAPTER 34, DAY 121, WOMEN

On day121 I tried to pick up where I left off at 3AM when the windows update ate my page on Costa Rican women. Of course it would never be the same. When I arrived here people would tell me about the insincere nature of the *Tico*. I thought it sounded very much like what passed for what I called friends back in the States.

When I arrived here I was also warned to watch out for the women. I was told to be careful and stuff like that. I always shrugged the warnings off with a nod, a smile and a laugh. I never understood what they meant. I always thought they were talking about gossiping or going after my money. I hadn't any interest in seeing which one it was and I thought I was sharp enough to stay safe.

I was busy homemaking and the immigration application was keeping me focused and I was not going to be sucked into anything. However, I remembered the warm feeling I felt from hanging out with the pocked faced chubby gal who showed me around on my exploratory trip a year earlier. Much of that feeling, I put off to being in Costa Rica and I gave appropriate weight on the fact that she could sit quietly and demand nothing. There was a beauty in that quietude that equaled the beauty of the smiles on her face. It was a quiet peace that stirred feelings of amour. I am talking about being in the state of love and not necessarily being in-love with someone.

Those beatific smiles were spawned by the deep sensual satisfaction of living in the tropics and the *Pura Vi*da mentality. That was especially true of the housecleaning gal. She knew how to make me laugh. I felt special around her and wanted for little else other than to hang out with her. That became apparent after our bus trip to the hardware store to shop for a ceiling fan. I finally comprehended what those guys meant by watch out for the women.

They could disarm me with their ready smiles and charm my pants off and the wallet out of my pocket. I did OK about keeping my pants on and the wallet in my pocket but that was the first time I had ever awoken at 1:00 AM thinking about someone I had not even flirted with. It wasn't infatuation, sex addiction or lust. She was just in my head and I could not fall back to sleep. An hour latter I rose out of bed and wrote.

To paraphrase that line from the song about werewolves in London: "She'll rip yer heart out Jim." The overwhelming desire to spend time with her had me terrified. What if we had become intimate? How would I ever be able to stop thinking about her? She was doing it without any deliberate intention because it was just who she was. (What was I saying about not becoming too intimate with people here?) However, maintaining distance in my relationships with others has never been in my nature.

In the States I was ready to write a screenplay about online dating after my experiences on a couple of dating sites. I remember that the gals who called themselves Buddhist all set a date to meet and then stopped communicating. The best reply I ever received from a Buddhist gal about that was "Just because I was not writing to you did not mean I was blowing you off." Women would collect long lists of "favorites" and never date any of the men they encouraged to write. Other women would collect first dates knowing that they were just looking seriously and not serious about their looking.

(My experiences with American women left me feeling sad. I was either sad for their lack of ability to share intimacy or sad for myself having unrequitedly shared so much of my own. In Costa Rica it was a whole new world of trouble.) In Costa Rica it all went back to the unworldly aspect of being here. This country was something I referred to as a spiritual vortex and being a matriarchal society the power lied in the women. Guys here know that and they kept a respectful distance by having casual sex and open filtrations. Intimacy and northern concepts of love were foreign here and the unwary had lost their hearts and had their wallets ripped out of their pants. I was glad for having that little taste of what to watch for but nothing could prepare me for the unexpected.

CHAPTER 35, DAY 124, MONEY

Day 124 brought me to thoughts of business. Being an organized and orderly type with a nervous nature I liked to have my business affairs in order. Somewhat old school and not very *Tico* I liked security. I had friends and businesses that assisted me from the States.

You need some facts if you think you are going to transition to a foreign country. Only after I sold my house and all but 500 lbs of personal possessions did I feel light enough to put my affairs in order. I had funeral plans and a burial plot in Oregon but I needed to decide if I was going to keep them or be buried afar. Because I was living alone business matters were a little complicated as to who would do what for me. One good suggestion was to hire a *Tico* lawyer to write a will and to be an emergency contact in Costa Rica.

That was low on my list of priorities and was only on my mind because of a mishap that could have been ugly. First I had found someone Stateside who would act as proxy in my business affairs. In hindsight, I would not pick a boy/girlfriend or former lover as there were too many emotional issues to contend with. If you were close with family or had trusted friends you could solicit one or two of them to help you.

I needed someone with power of attorney for all my financial affairs. I also needed someone to execute my Directives to Physicians. And I needed someone to execute my will as well as a will or trust. It could be something as simple as "I leave everything toward the care and feeding of my favorite feline friend Felix who is in the care of my cousin Connie. The residue of the estate I bequeath to Connie." All those forms are available in Stevens Ness forms that can be purchased in many stationary stores in the US.

I opened some joint bank accounts so different friends could access my funds and wire money if needed. With residency and house buying I had needed that help. To reduce liability I opened a small joint account into which I could online transfer funds from my main individual account. My important papers were kept in a joint safe deposit box that also had to be accessed for banking documents. I also needed a way to stay in touch with the people and businesses in the north.

With a laptop and internet access I did my banking and checked on credit cards online which eliminated the need for paper statements. I set up my credit cards to be paid automatically out of one of my bank accounts. I then could buy online and not worry about when the statements needed to be paid. I just needed to be sure there was money in the account. This was not enough because I eventually needed to talk to someone about the online glitches.

I bought and brought a Magic Jack from Radio Shack. It worked through the internet and for $20 a year I had unlimited toll free calling to the US and. To use the Magic Jack I needed online service and for $20 a month I purchased enough signal to use the phone and to open and download small files. Minimally I needed a laptop or notebook. I did not have to pack up a mammoth desk unit and ship it.

I also bought a Lonely Planet guide book to Costa Rica and a waterproof map. I hear they are available at Barnes and Nobel. And for the rainy afternoons you would wish you brought a waterproof day bag and a good vented collapsible umbrella like the ones for sale at AAA, Eddie Bauer or Target Stores. Rubber boots were recommended for jungle hikes as protection from snake bites. You see some of the old-timers here wearing rubber boots in town.

CHAPTER 36, DAY 125, *TICO* WORDS

On day 125 words kept coming to mind. I thought about the words that were common here which I had adopted and those which I had yet to incorporate into my lexicon. Last time I wrote about hello and now I'll address good bye. *Adios* was common here but rarely used as a closing salutation. More commonly *Hasta Luego* (Until later) was used alone. The girls liked to say *Ciao*; sometimes I'd hear *'Luego*. Once I heard a bus driver call to a departing rider "*Adios, hasta luego, tiene un buen dia.*" I liked "have a good day." Of course there was the omnipresent *Pura Vida* and it was the greeting for all occasions. I did not mention that hellos were often a long strung out affair with a mix of *Pura Vidas, Buenas dias, Como estas, Que tal* and/or *Como la va*.

Asi es was becoming more and more a part of my prater and I was making an effort to use *Pura Vida*. It was always safe to repeat what the greeter had offered you and sometimes my same greetings were repeated back to me. I also practiced *Si, pero no* frequently. As in Japan, it was impolite to say no or to refuse an offering. Often the subject was just changed or an excuse was offered without using the word no. An expression unique to Costa Rica was "Yes, but no." As in "Yes, I would have loved a cup of coffee but no I would not accept your offer because it was too late in the day for me to be drinking coffee."

Muchisimas gracias was another phrase I had only heard here. Like *muchas graci*as it means thank you but with an "so very much" attached to it. The Costa Ricans really liked to use diminutive forms of speech. A local gal told me that painting the roof was a *quierocito* (a little want) the kind of thing you might like but not really need. (It was true I could have lived without painting the roof.) Also *cafecito* (little coffee) was another word for a cup of coffee.

One of my all time favorite expressions, because of its historical origin, was *matando la culeba*. When the sugar cane plantation owners would check the workers and see there was little done that phrase was the ready excuse. The workers would say that they were busy "killing the snake" and that was why they had not been cutting cane. It's comparable to the northern "killing time" except you were paid for it. The being paid for it part was the aspect a *Tica* friend was quick to point out to me.

I mentioned *Que me importa?* in earlier pages and it was worth mentioning again. I would have done well to think more often in terms of "What does that have to do with me." That thinking was so prevalent here they even had a second expression I*MMMMmmmporta a me?* This has the same meaning.

There were a plethora of wishy washy expressions or expressions that relinquished responsibility. Some often heard expressions included: *Mas o menos; Quen sabe,* and; *Tal ves.* More or less, who knows and maybe were used often. When responding to *Como estas?* (How is it?) it was often *Bien gracias a Dios* (Good, thanks to God) or *Muy bien por dicha*: (Very good luckily). When people scheduled a meeting it was most often dependent on *Que los Dios quire,* (What the Gods like).

Latin thinking was also revealed in the words for time. *Ahora* could mean now, in a little while or soon. *Ya* also meant right away, already, or later; which the user intended I would find out later. I am going to do that right away might mean when I get around to it. I already did it could mean I am going to get around to it someday.

An expression I learned in the Rosetta Stone program that I liked was *Encontado de conoserlo*. It was not used here but was such an elegant way of saying Enchanted to meet you. The typical response was *Equal*. *Equal* was used to say; same to you. Also, *Equal* was often used to return a salutation like have a nice day, Good afternoon, etc.

CHAPTER 37 DAY 126, BUSINESS

On day 126 my mind was back on business because there were a few more business concerns I hadn't covered earlier.

An address in the USA...I don't know where you live if you don't live anywhere. I always had P.O. Boxes and even that was not an adequate solution because they only forwarded for a limited time. I was looking into a mail forwarding service and eventually that could be a good option. If I was not living in the States and could pick any address I was going to pick a State with no income taxes. My income may leave me with no tax to pay but I might still need to file and maybe pay for tax prep.

For the first few months I used a friend's address. I trusted that friend to hold and not destroy my mail or pilfer through it. However, in a not that uncommon female emotional moment, one friend threatened to drop off my box of mail and important papers at another friend's house. I did not need that kind of stress. I would suggest finding a way to the keep business strictly business.

If I did change States I would have to contend with driver's licenses and/or ID cards. I did not plan to drive in Costa Rica but I needed to rent and drive cars on trips in the US. To obtain a license or ID I would need a physical address. Buying a forwarding service and changing my mailing address often does not provide a physical address. I would keep my Oregon license until it expired and keep paying the insurance on the truck I did not own anymore because it was cheaper than paying for insurance on a two week car rental.

Another bit of business I had to contend with was flying. I hope you like air travel. As much as it pollutes our lungs and punches more holes in the ozone the planes were flying with me or without me. What airline to fly depended on what you needed? I needed to lug a bunch of baggage and Continental/United was my carrier of choice because of their generous baggage allowances.

I could fly much cheaper by making multiple stops or by changing carriers. I was paying $700 for a round trip with one stop that continued on the same carrier. I paid an extra $230 to have 250 pounds of luggage flown to Costa Rica. True I could have flown for between $300 and $500 but that would have required changing airlines mid trip, having multiple layovers, higher baggage fees, spending more time in the air, and/or having extra long layovers. I saw one flight for sale that took 31 hours when 11 to 13 hour trips were common with a 2 to 3 hour layover. Eventually I bought my flights about four months in advance and directly from the airline website to get the best price.

There was also the question of one-way versus round trip. If I knew that THIS WAS IT I might have considered a one-way trip. I was surprised to find that comparable one way flights were more expensive than round trip tickets. Actually it was cheaper to buy a round trip and burn the return flight. I was told that buying a fully refundable ticket gives the option to cash it in but I generally did not find those in my online shopping. Someday, I might call and check on refundable tickets but by then I should be flying carry on only and could just buy a cheap flight with multiple carriers.

Here was a bit of banking info I neglected to mention earlier. When I opened my joint accounts I asked for two ATM cards. I brought both because if I lost one it would be hell to replace and the one I carried was the one in my friend's name. If I lost that card and the copy of my passport that I carried the finder would not have an ATM card and ID with matching names.

I did not want to carry my passport around with me and I had the photo page color copied the size of a business card laminated it to carry in my wallet. It was good ID and accepted everywhere except the bank, hospital, border crossings or when driving a car. I left my original passport somewhere safe. Unless I was going to the bank I did not carry my ATM card with me. I knew a guy who lived here who lost two ATM cards in as many months and had trouble obtaining cash until a new one came.

If you could remember every credit card number, three digit code, expiration date, ATM card number, bank account number, checking account and routing number, insurance policy number and the phone numbers to call them, your online log-ins and passwords for all the above, and all your ID and passport numbers, and the addresses and phone numbers of all your friends, and their passport numbers; then you are better than I. It was something I wanted and something I would not want someone else to find. Making a paper copy made the most sense to me.

I put these numbers, and every important number and password on a piece of paper and guarded it with my life. Someone suggested that I email myself a copy. However, after I discussed the idea with a friend words like spyware, malware, key logger and hard drive vulnerability were mentioned. Saving on disk, flash drive and paper were suggestions from someone more computer savvy than I. I was too old school to trust having internet access when I needed it or that it could not be hacked and reallllyyyy bad people would now have MY ENTIRE ID.

If relocating or just visiting there are some money concerns you might consider: Do you own dollars? Do you have money in the bank? Do you have enough cash to pay for all the incidentals of your trip? If you answered yes to all three questions leave your cash at home in your interest bearing account.

Bring your ATM card and credit card and **notify the bank and credit card company that you will be in Costa Rica**. Ask the bank to increase your ATM limit to $600 so you can withdraw as much cash as possible in one transaction and minimize your transaction fees. Have the credit card company ask the fraud dept to not to hold up charges to your card while you travel.

That said I avoided using credit cards as it was inviting fraud, double billing and identity theft. You might not be able to obtain $600 in local cash (300,000.00 Colones) from the ATM at one time but it is worth trying. You could always take less. When traveling I carried a couple hundred US bucks for the US incidentals at the airport and such. They took dollars here at stores and hotels but would hurt you on the exchange rates. The ATM gives you the current bank exchange rate and there is no standing in line at the bank to change cash or to cash checks. Check with your bank for fees and charges that might apply.

There were many books on Costa Rica and I had seen plenty of them. If you were going to Barnes and Noble for the waterproof Costa Rica map you want to buy the Lonely Planet, or Moon book on Costa Rica. Other books had some other interesting material but I feel the Lonely Planet book was best overall. I read and highlighted information that mattered to me before planning my literary and brought it with me.

The residency laws changed March 1, 2010 and Costa Rican residency was no longer cheaper than many other Latin American countries. Prior to that date I could not meet the residency requirements in many of those other places. Now I would not even be an acceptable residency applicant in Costa Rica. However, it would be cheaper to live almost anywhere else in Latin America. If you had the money to meet residency requirements elsewhere you could find a comparable climate and less expensive living.

CHAPTER 38, DAY 129, YOUR ARRIVAL

On day 129 it felt like there was something weird about writing to an imaginary audience. I talked about my landing here but I never explained what you might expect at the airport. Do you have a friend here with a car? That was really the best way to travel if they are an experienced Costa Rica driver. They were crazy drivers in Costa Rica and I preferred the bus or taxi. If a friend could meet you at the airport with a taxi it costs less because the taxi needs to run both ways and city taxis have a cheaper rate than airport taxis. If you land alone you would need Colones and transportation. You can avoid the *Casa De Cambio* (House of Change) inside the terminal and use the ATM right outside the terminal exit where you will be accosted by gypsy and metered taxi drivers. Withdraw 200,000.00 Colones (about $400.00) before you get a cab so the meter is not running but take your bags with you to the ATM.

You will want to avoid the gypsy cabs and find a metered cab by asking "*Usted tiene una Maria?*" The airport taxi meter started at 775 or something like that. You want to be sure it was reset so you are not paying for who knows what. It was usual and customary for men traveling alone to sit up front with the driver and practice a little Spanish. Women and couples generally sit in the back seat. If you are going to San Jose, Alajuela or Heredia the driver might know his way around those areas.

If going to a distant destination or small town instruct the taxi to drop you at the park and then you can take a local cab to your ultimate destination. The flag fee will be worth the time saved wandering around or asking for directions. Once the meter is running time is money. Once at your destination you need to look at the meter and ask if that is the fare to pay. The meters jumps in odd intervals and just chatting or taking the bags out can cost you.

The buses are great here but they take a little planning. The Monte Verde web site had a comprehensive schedule. With the bus stop locations in San Jose from the Lonely Planet book and a little planning you could go anywhere in Costa Rica on inexpensive clean public transportation. You still might want to take a cab out of the airport even if it is to go to a bus stop. If it were early in the day you could take an Alajuela bus from the airport and catch a bus to your destination by walking between bus terminals.

Bring everything that you think you might want for your visit. Otherwise the items you might want could be either hard to find or very expensive. Check with your airline for charges and offer to bring your friends some special items they also might like. I could go on and on about what was expensive and what was worth the two dollar a pound baggage charge or about items I just could not find here. (You will want your specialty items from the US; you just do not know what specialty items are yet.)

I paid extra baggage charges just to have certain items from the States. If you don't bring it yourself you must forego expecting others to bring it or have it for you.

Captain was a world traveler and he said "Get an Iphone." Small and light and it would serve you anywhere there was wifi. Roger says, "Buy the Acer notebook with windows 7." He was buying one for me to pick up in April. I liked my Magic Jack and many others seemed to be using it here. Some preferred Skype because of the video capability but the bandwidth of Skype and the dropping of calls had me give up on it. There was also Yahoo and Windows messengers once you have an internet connection.

Used, worn and ordinary looking items are less of a target for would-be thieves. I dress down on purpose. Depending on how you do with the sun or if you plan to visit the jungles or stay out after dark will help you decide about long pants. A light water repellant jacket would be nice if you were going to visit rainforests. Some mountain towns cool off dramatically in the PM and a breathable sweater is a must. There are many climates here and if you travel you could experience super hot, to very cool and wet, or dry and windy. It was humid almost everywhere so it is best to bring clothes that dry fast.

CHAPTER 39, DAY 133, PAT AND MIKE

Day 133 was Saint Patty's Day and a "Top o' the mornin'" wish to you all and just to complete the salute… "And the rest of the day to you kind sir."

May St. Pat drive all the snakes from your island wherever it tis. I hope you had a corned beef and cabbage and tossed back some Guinness or Bass and washed it down with a bit of Jamison's for me. (Now, Mike was seen peeing over the grave of his good friend Pat. Mary, who had witnessed the act, asked him "Mike" she said "Since you and Pat were such good friends why were ya out there pissin' on his grave?" Mike was quick to answer in a slurred tone "I'd promised Pat I'd pour a bottle o' whiskey o'r his grave after he was gone and… and I didn't think he'd mind a bit if I passed it through me kidneys first.")

It was the middle of summer here in terms of heat. Yesterday it was 97 degrees in the heat of the day. In Oregon I would be dying. Here it was only 10 to 17 degrees above the norm. It did cool off in the PM and night and that was the saving grace. Global warming has the tropics heating up steadily and it was hotter and dryer than in past years. May 15 it will start to rain every day and temperatures will simmer-down.

(The lull in my writing was brought on by a low in my life. I had been struggling with a thorny personal problem related to family. I don't have much family so any family problem involves a big part of my familial experience.) Expatriates all find new family upon embarking upon their adventure. If you go off to your new country with spouse and youngins your new brothers and cousins were a strange lot. There were your fellow countrymen who escaped from the motherland and the culturally alien natives of your new homeland. When one embarked on that kind of journey they were in a whole new relationship with the universe?

I want to send any would-be travelers and expats to a web site to which a dear friend sent me. At the International Center for Education, University of California at Irvine there was a search bar up on the top of the home page. When I searched for "how to prepare," I found an index bar on the left that covered health, safety, money and most importantly cultural adjustment. This is all great information and filled with more links to other information.

I was writing more of a diary or log they had more of a how-to manual on their site. It validated much of my experience and reminded me of aspects of moving here I had neglected to cover. For example: I never told you I received Hepatitis A and B shots and other preparatory measures that are worth knowing. The site was geared toward student travelers and was somewhat theoretical but worth visiting. It was not the answer to everything but it was a great source and put emphasis on what you SHOULD do and not what the writer has done.

I send people there because the site is so patronizing. Somebody needed to tell ya what to do and it just isn't my style. I was happy to just keep observing and reporting. I intended to spend some time studying that site and creating a few pages of "How-to" myself. I had been shorting you with stories of antics and not providing you with a guide to heaven. Ha ha ha...

Moreover, all the greats will tell you that heaven is in your mind. Well, your mind is in your body and you must take care of that first if you think you are going to travel to the mystical mountains of your mind. Expatriating was a mystical experience. How did Jim, a *Gringo* and a former hotel neighbor, put it? You will never be more alone in your life or more reliant on yourself for everything. He theorized it was the cause of the spiritual awakening that awaits the expat. It was an open door to that which was holy inside of you. It was a chance not only to see God but to sit down for a visit and chat about what is and what was and what will be.

CHAPTER 40, DAY 134, LIVING *GRINGO* STYLE

On day 134 I was another day closer to my five month anniversary. Before I knew it I would be receiving my One Year pin. I was getting closer to being settled in my home. Yard work was started in earnest as I dug out unwanted plants and transplanted others. I looked for the underground utilities and dug in the thatched grass.

There was so much that was becoming common place for me and didn't seem significant enough to share but you would have liked to have known. There were snippets of exchanges with *Gringos*; new *Tico* relations, more retail experiences, home making, heart breaking and the culture, the culture.

I said I fell for the puff pieces in the literature about Costa Rica and here was a commonly used piece of fluff "I moved here for the weather but I love it here because of the people." Whatever the source it was probably just one person who said those words 30 years ago and every other book quotes that book. Most *Gringos* isolated themselves from Costa Ricans and hung out in little lily white clutches clucking about the conditions that surrounded them.

They lived in massive homes in the hills. They drove big four wheel drive SUVs to town daily and sought out *Gringo* friends. They spoke little Spanish and were waiting for the *Ticos* to attain a higher level of Americanism. They insisted that Costa Rica would turn into small town USA. soon and they would then feel more comfortable. They steadfastly ignored the culture in which they were living and for as long as they had been here and as hard as they tried the *Ticos* still didn't speak English. (I actually heard that comment about speaking English from a *Gringo*.)

Not only did these *Gringos* isolate themselves from the *Ticos* but they seemed cold and clickish and did not embrace the cultural etiquette. They were not happy, friendly or outgoing. They were slow to extend their hands and hadn't the courtesy to introduce themselves when given an introduction. I assumed that they must have been *muy importante* (very important) people.

One fellow had been living here seven years and did not know that the prevailing wage in the area was two dollars an hour. In his arrogance and disrespect he offered a *Tico* six dollars an hour to help him shop for a rental house. The *Tico* was insulted by that garish display of wealth and referred to his employer as a *"pinche Gringo."* The *Tico* also took a one hundred dollar deposit on an art commission from the arrogant sot and may very well have stiffed him? The *Tico* was already not showing up for scheduled meetings. The *Gringo* called it a "rip-off." I say "You reap what you sow."

Not that I care. *Que me importa*? (Why were they here? Did they move to a country full of brown people to wait for them to turn white?) They complained that the locals were not changing fast enough. And many *Gringos* kept an unhealthy distance from the people they lived amongst. Maybe I cared because it reflected badly on me. I was now clumped into the group of Ugly Americans and was an equally worthy target for scorn or pandering.

As for rip-offs, my roof painting friend took three dollars and sixty cents from my change box when we were working. First, he took a five mill bill and replaced it with a one mill bill. As we continued to work there was not going to be enough money in the tin to pay him for the day. Then he put another two mill bill in the tin so I had enough to pay him for the day. The end result was that he took five mill and replaced it with three mill and lost all my trust and respect.

In a related story, the cleaning lady would say I was rich. And for the longest time I could not find one plastic drinking tumbler and one soup mug that was a gift from my deceased mother. After a year passed I finally let myself believe she took it. I guess it was worth all the other work I could provide or the referrals I could send her. I was looked at as part of a group of people who had not earned respect because of a lack of offering respect. Try as I might I would always be white. (Forget the fact that most Costa Ricans considered themselves white and did have fair skin.)

CHAPTER 41, DAY 136, SPIRITUAL EXPERIENCE

On day 136 I asked "Who needed trust?" Trust required prescribed outcomes. I was trying for having faith. With faith anything could happen and it would all be good. It will probably take until my death to discover how to truly love other human beings. But this was a process and not an individual act or a state of mind. Many authors suggested I follow my bliss or they wrote how they found their bliss. No one ever wrote about how hard it was to accept bliss. Someone should have warned me about the difficulty and fear I would discover in bliss.

I felt that pure bliss was not fit for human consumption. It was meant for pure spirit because the body had too many frailties to accept such a gift. My reaction was as far beyond fear as bliss was beyond happiness. It could only be described as terror. (Why would I shun bliss? Easy...it was just not familiar.) It was beyond odd and I found it unacceptably foreign to me. I found many ways to reject or destroy bliss. If I tried to hold on to it, it forced me to face the unknown and to shed those aspects of myself I considered being part of me. Bliss was a new reality that required the release of everything I believed to be real and correct. It did not seem like any part of my known reality. I just wanted to know when I could come down to the tainted images that I held on to as being my reality. What was familiar and what I thought was real was what the Buddhists referred to as illusion.

I had read and thought on many topics. I walked and I thought, I sat and I thought, I felt and I thought, I acted and I thought. Many revelations were presented to me and many insights were offered. Many psychic and spiritual opportunities were laid out before me. I was allowed to surf in the clouds. I felt the breath of God. I was given a chance to see the world and every place in it.

Today my eyes were opened to the magic moment. There was only now. I suffered from illusion and fantasy and had projected and anticipated a future. That was the type of thinking that spawned desire. Desire, the Buddhists said, was the cause of all pain. Perhaps anticipation was the seat of disappointment.

That morning I felt reborn into a world where I could not be hurt because in the now there was only what is and there were no thoughts or plans for what will be. From here everything seemed much clearer. I could see you and I could see me in total truth and honesty. I was here and you were there. There was no such thing as together; there were only individual beings of light on their respective paths. From my isolated perch I could love in perfect safety. I could acknowledge the separation that exists between us and view life with perfect detachment. Whatever might have happened and/or could happen did not serve me in the moment. Nothing happened in heaven, there were only peace, quiet and stillness. I felt no joy and I felt no pain. There was no want and there was no desire, so it followed that there was no disappointment.

I was blessed with a kind of freedom that I had forgotten. I was alone but not lonely. I was full of love and loved no one. Everything was possible and nothing was probable. My mind, body and spirit were unshackled from the deception of illusion and I was free to live life in just moments that unfolded before me. I was opened to what God had put before me and I made no plans and there were no desired outcomes.

I had forgotten why I was here in the land of "in the moment." Tomorrow there was only tomorrow. And I was capable of falling into the *pinche Gringo* trap of looking for the world to fit my image and waiting in inane ignorance for it to happen. I supposed I only disliked the *Gringos* because they reminded me of... me.

Nevertheless, I was here to practice releasing my dogged attachment to my own limited vision of perfection. I was not sure what I was doing here. Maybe I was on a spiritual quest but I did not know what I was looking for? Perhaps I was surrounded by saints traveling incognito and I was just too blind to see them.

CHAPTER 42, DAY 140, HUMAN EXPERIENCE

On day 140 I had been told I had a sour attitude and that my bad humor was showing in my writing. I thought I was writing of hazards and pitfalls for other would-be-expatriates to avoid. There was a request for more beauty and allure. I guessed that each of my readers wanted something different. I only knew what I wanted to write. How much anyone took from what I wrote was dependent on their attitude as a reader and not my attitude as a writer.

For those of you who might need a change of perspective from my doom, gloom and depression... buy a tour book to read along side of this tome. For me to write a fluffy puff piece I would only have to cut and paste what has been written a hundred times. I was attempting to offer some new insight and to inspire intuition. I was looking to provide the reader a guide to easy living in Costa Rica... living being the operative word. A guide for a tourist adventure written by tourists for tourists was easily available at your local bookstore, library or here on the internet.

I was not a tourist and this story was not a Hollywood movie. I remembered that when I moved to San Francisco I did not visit North Beach, Fisherman's Wharf, Coit Tower or the museums or zoo. However, I really did enjoy riding my Triumph 650 through Golden Gate Park, past the beach, around the Presidio and Fort Point to loop back to my home on Page Street. Other than that, I remembered fog and cold and working a dull job.

When I lived two hours away from "The City" I went to the Tea Gardens, art museum, cultural events and other touristy stuff. I guess if I lived in the US I would visit the cloud forest, waterfall parks, beaches, volcanoes and other tourist destinations of Costa Rica. But I did not live in the US and was not pouring over tour books looking for the strange and interesting places to see here in Costa Rica.

I went to the bank yesterday and that was the highlight of my day. I was elated and exhausted at the end of my experience and cannot describe to you the deep sense of satisfaction I felt. I had opened my online access and had three utility bills set up on auto-pay. I did not understand all the particulars of the set-up and cannot gain access to my accounts through my laptop but the clerk commented that I was as *Tico* as *Gallo Pinto*. That was a high compliment for a *Gringo*. *Gallo Pinto* was local rice and bean dish served with most meals and was a symbol for *Tico* culture. What a day! I went to a *soda* to celebrate with a *casado* for lunch

There were beautiful parks and forests to enjoy just a short bus ride from town. I needed to do little more than look out my window to see natural beauty. Every walk to town was filled with wonder. Every moment working in the yard was communion with God. (Did you all really want to hear about that stuff? Every book I ever picked up about Costa Rica was full of that dribble.)

CHAPTER 43, DAY 141, FURNITURE SHOPPING

Day 141 and my less than Pollyanna perspective drives my fingers forward on the keys to flesh out another story of truth and beauty. If this was beautiful was up to the reader to decide. I told this story on the phone a few times and it felt like I had written it but I hadn't. I had been sleeping on a wooden framed cot and sitting on plastic chairs and enjoying a plywood table supported by two five gallon paint cans. Very *Tico* perhaps but most *Ticos* had much nicer furnishings than I had. I was trying to live inexpensively and was in no hurry to furnish the place.

An online friend accepted an invitation to visit and I had been planning to buy a real bed for myself so they could have the twin bed. A table and chairs for eating might also be nice and maybe some simple furnishings for the *sala* (living room). So I set out to shop for the type and price range of furniture I might like. I was a walker so I knew where the furniture stores were in town. I wanted to keep my money local even though everyone suggested I go to Sarchie (famous for hand crafted furniture) or San Jose (the big city) to buy. There were seven stores in town and two on the outskirts and a few department stores with the odd piece or two. I felt content to shop in Grecia if I found what I wanted and I could afford it.

All the stores had the prices marked on the furniture and often the clerk offered me an immediate discount of eight or nine percent. I found that if I pushed I received a 10 percent discount easy enough. I was told before leaving Oregon that the Latin people respected a good negotiator and haggling over the price was both good business and good manners. People said that paying full price was a garish display of wealth and showed distain for interacting with the shop keeper.

So, off I went with pen and pad in hand. I was listing pieces and prices and noting styles and discount offers. Eventually I found a store that had most of the pieces I wanted and what he didn't have he offered to order. I like to think of my caution as prudence and not paranoia and I tried to keep the deposit low and the discount high.

From the day that I shopped to the day that I ordered two chairs from a four-piece table and chair set were sold. The eating table I wanted had only been seen in another store and I was counting on this shop to order it. The manager wanted a 50% deposit. Well, that was a $400 deposit on an $800 order and a lot of money for me to lose if things went wrong. Faith prevailed and I agreed to place the order. We needed to agree on how big a discount I was going to receive for ordering all the pieces from him.

I was paying cash and I figured a 20% discount would be possible. Ten percent was offered and I countered with fifteen. We settled on twelve percent discount and then the fun began. Figures couldn't lie but liars could figure. He punched a bunch of keys in the calculator and showed me a number that he said was 12%. I wasn't everybody's fool and I immediately saw that it was less than a 10% discount. But he was eager to shake on it. We went back and forth for a long time discussing mathematical theory and practice until finally I broke it down to moving decimal points. You know, move it once for 10% then move it twice for 1% and add the 10% and two 1%'s to result in 12%. Those basic calculations were done on paper and trumped the fancy fingering on the calculator. I had secured a good price and we both had smiles and handshakes as he took the deposit and he offered a receipt. I walked away with a promise for delivery in seven days for all the furniture that was ordered…

There was a little back and forth about the delivery and we were still short the two chairs that went with the four-piece set. I waited for a half-hour for the truck with the eating table and chairs to load and deliver the bed and mattress. Eventually all but four pieces were delivered and I had to go back the next day to increase my deposit and was gifted three wooden bowls in appreciation of my business. I was moved by the gesture and looked forward to receiving my other pieces. I felt blessed for the early advice, my math skills and meeting these kind folks. In the end he did get the better of me on the two chairs that went with the four piece set. When the two chairs arrived they were seconds with blemishes, the wrong color and the wood panels in the chairs were of different tones. Oh well, It's Costa Rica! Ha ha ha. I accepted them as they were.

CHAPTER 44, DAY 164, CULTURE SHOCK

Day 164 was the third day I had been back to Costa Rica from Oregon. (Did I neglect to say I was leaving town? I guess so! My fingers were even rusty having taken so much time off from writing.) I was happy to say I did not miss writing but here I was again writing.

What could have been harder than leaving your home country to live in a foreign land? The answer was (drum roll please!) you are not going to believe this, and it was… going back to your home country. Once I heard a mother forgive her twenty something son for swearing at her with "He just came back from living in a foreign land." A veteran expatriate gal Jan who sold in Grecia's farmers' market said that the culture shock of going back to the States was much worse than the shock of leaving and I agreed.

I just returned from two weeks in Oregon and it was one of the most difficult transitions I had ever made. Not so much coming back to Costa Rica, it was going to the US that was so difficult. Of course the people who lived the US and had not expatriated had no idea what I was talking about.

Oregon was beautiful and I moved there because of the scenic beauty. However, transitioning from walking everywhere to driving 70 miles an hour was strange. That alone was indicative of the difference in pace. All my friends wanted attention and I thought I was on a business trip. My friends did not understand that I had a lot of business I wanted to take care of. Clerks and strangers often seemed rude compared to Costa Ricans and the size of the stores and the glare of the lights was unsettling.

I loved my friends and wanted to spend time with them and there was so much to do on a two week business trip. Both the business and the friends uncovered feelings and sensations that had seemingly been forgotten. Frustrations and anxieties I had not felt for five months were bigger and bolder than ever. Everything seemed so much more daunting. However, the food was great and I enjoyed the variety and familiarity of the foods available. Shopping was also much easier on familiar ground and with the labels in English.

I visited some beautiful places, and saw some wonderful people. I was able to bring a little Pura Vida back to the States with me and it attracted outstanding moments like the magnet. I may have been driving fast but I had slowed down a lot. I certainly had a more relaxed outlook toward the events and exchanges than the former me.

Back in Costa Rica with four suitcases of trinkets and devices to put away or install, I had more business to attend to than before I had left. I also had to adjust to Costa Rica again. Once there was food in the house and some things put away and a few friends contacted I felt home again.

There was a certain beauty and softness in Costa Rican interactions that was missing in the US. In Costa Rica there was a certain small town feeling of support and the scenic beauty here was unparalleled anywhere else. Don't get me wrong, I am certain that wherever you live is a beautiful place to be. In Costa Rica I was not going to be able to walk around in fresh snow and feel the gentle white snowflakes falling on my face.

I will know what to expect next time I go north and that will make it a little easier... The next time I would be prepared for the transition in culture before I left. And when you lived in Costa Rica you had to go somewhere for vacation!

CHAPTER 45, DAY 171, GREEN SEASON

Day 171 was a Saturday and a farmer's market day. I had been back in Costa Rica a little over a week and was still readjusting. I had set up a few of my electronic toys and I had done grocery shopping and a few loads of laundry. But I felt down. Maybe it was the weight of the business that was so heavy? Maybe it was the personal stuff that was started in the US that was weighing me down? Maybe it was the re-realization that I lived in a foreign country that was so crushing? Then again maybe it was just that *invierno* had come on completely that was so daunting?

Winter is what you call it. The rainy season was what the locals called it in English. *Invierno* was not like the winter I knew in the north. It was the season of greening as warm rains fell most afternoons. It would rain for an hour or so. These were hard rains that soaked you to the bone in five minutes. The rains came and went and many locals carried umbrellas or stood under shelter until the squall passed.

The days were graying. The early mornings were overcast turning to sunshine long enough to evaporate the ground water that then formed clouds that dropped the afternoon rains. It might have been gray, but it was still very bright and warm. It was in the high 70's to low 80's and the level of humidity rose as the rains continued. I had noticed the molds beginning to grow on the sidewalks.

Everything will eventually be verdant in response to the frequent wetting. Anywhere the algae-like green had taken hold would be watered into life again. Trees were abloom with new vigor as they received a good dose of water. New leaves and growth were filling the branches and the vistas. This was the opposite of the Northern deciduous trees that shed their leaves in the winter; Costa Rican deciduous trees shed their leaves in the summer to conserve water and leaf out in the winter

On that day I felt like I did not fit in anywhere. The States seemed foreign to me and so did Costa Rica. Costa Rica should feel foreign as it was a country with different values, customs and language than where I grew up.

I seemed to be craving more *Gringo* contact than I had before I left for Oregon. I talked on the phone to the States more often and visited my *Gringo* friends here more often than had before I had left for the north. I had even taken to making tourist trips with Jim. Thankfully he was willing to take the local buses to visit out of the way places and walk some short distances. Jim and I had a symbiotic relationship as he had visited some spots already and we shared the cost of transportation. He might have felt more secure because my Spanish skills were better than his and he really craved company.

We went to a waterfall park a half-hour bus ride from Grecia. The waterfall park was a five dollar taxi ride from the bus stop and had a six dollar entry fee. At the park there was a half-hour walk down hill through a manicured jungle trail to the creek and pool that caught the falls. There was a short walk up a side creek went to another falls but Jim was not too adventurous.

We also took a ride to San Isidro to visit John at the house which I stayed at when I first arrived. Grecia was considered to be within the central valley but it was built on a bench on the top of a ridge line. So the two mile by two mile town center was surrounded by ridgeline roads going both up and down into the suburbs. San Isidro was one of those suburbs and would more correctly be called San Isidro de Grecia. Like most of the suburbs, San Isidro had its own church, school, park, store, restaurant, bar and not much more. Some of these *barrios* (neighborhoods) had more services and shops than others and there was no apparent reason for this. Some had clinics; stores, pharmacies and an ATM or bank and some others had little more than a church, park and maybe a store.

CHAPTER 46, DAY 174, LUGGAGE

It was day 174 when I had been back for almost two weeks and the house felt less cluttered and chaotic. Some projects like the Acer notebook, the router and the solar shop light had resigned themselves to future projects. The fact that things were put away or just working made me feel a little more settled. One unsettling event that I had been allowing to occupy my mind was that my luggage was pilfered in transit.

TSA had plausible deniability and the Airline blamed TSA. TSA, for those of you who do not use air travel much, are the airport people who check luggage and passengers for the airport's security. To that end, they keep security cameras focused on the people who bring luggage to the inspection station. Once the luggage is at the inspection station the luggage and inspector are hidden from camera and who knows what happens during the inspection process...

Here was another travel tip: buy TSA locks so they don't have to tear your luggage apart causing irreparable damage. Next, have someone else stand with your luggage at the belt feeding the x-ray machine so you can watch it come off the belt (or vice a versa). Then it either goes to the airplane or to the inspection station. This is an important point; you have the right to witness any inspection of your luggage. Tell the primary handler that you insist on witnessing any inspection and you are waiting nearby if there are any questions. I would also advise putting a packing list in your bags. The note may not save you from pilferage but it might cause some agent or ground crew member to think twice.

When you have arrived at your destination you need to check the condition of your bags and the contents. You would have to return to the airport if a damage report was necessary. Avoid the temptation to leave the situation you have just been in for the last 14 to 16 hours and just spend another hour or two finding someone to file a report.

Once your precious belongings are gone, they are gone. A belt accident, baggage mishandling, TSA, or a passerby at the carrousel while you are in line at immigration... anything could happen. Rumor had it that Airline and TSA claims were regularly denied so be sure you read any contract of cartage or baggage agreement the airline might have. I began a claim about my loss but I abandoned the process because it would have only been more hurtful for me to spend my time with a claim just to be told <u>one more time</u> that "Our employees don't steal." I guessed that my missing belongings were an act of God.

(Well, that was enough good advice for one page, so let me address the weather). There finally was some weather. The rains usually fell between 1:00 PM and 2:00 PM and might last an hour *mas o menos* (more or less). Sometimes it rained through the evening and night or there were more short squalls. Sometimes it seemed like the clouds just exploded all of a sudden and dropped a huge load of heavy drops. There might have been some sprinkles as a warning but when it rained it rained hard. The first storm I walked in I had a Dollar Store umbrella and that left me soaked and left the umbrella broken and in the trash.

The local people had enough sense to just stay out of the rain. When it rained the streets were almost deserted and people were lurking in doorways watching the event. People walking seemed to pick up their lazy Costa Rican pace and the drivers were just as oblivious to pedestrians as they were when the weather was clear.

There could be thunder and lightning and rain in big drops. It was gray most mornings and I now carried a $20 umbrella made by Tote's and sold at Target. That was a world class umbrella. For people expatriating to the tropics and those who might walk in the rain... Buy one!

CHAPTER 47, DAY 175, HOUSING

Day 175 had a beautiful sunny morning and the birds that woke me in the morning were happily continuing their songs outside the window. Ahhh Paradise. Most mornings were rain free if not downright sunny and warm. They say "A sunny morning is food for afternoon rains."

I loved my life here and I was realistic about the fact that everything changed. For example, the lush green hillside I viewed from the laundry window turned into a clear cut and might eventually be covered with houses. The city will become less inviting and scarier and so it goes no matter where you live. It was almost spooky to return and visit Los Angeles California after leaving my childhood home there. In my mid-twenties I moved to the more friendly environs north of San Francisco and when I visited LA it was not the same.

The Costa Rican suburbs were more likely to maintain their peaceful feeling. The strings of homes that lined the roads to and from the hills leave little space for development to take root. I would see more change here in town than those who lived out of town. I lived in what might be referred to as row housing. *Me barrio* was a series of small lots with houses packed closely together. Most of the houses had joining walls that helped keep the cost of construction down. It was government low income housing. My little house has only walls separating the residences and I just prayed for good neighbors. My prayers were answered and except for the occasional late night party this is a quiet, peaceful neighborhood.

I should mention the 100 to 300 thousand dollar houses that brightened the night time view of the hills. There were a few two thousand and three thousand square foot homes with enough lighting to land a helicopter. Be American, buy American and pay American prices for services. I had heard of $200 a month electric bills being paid by those who wanted all the toys and gadgets they enjoyed in the States. (Why would you not have a solar battery charger on the electric gate in a land where the sun shines almost daily?)

I had shown Jim a couple of houses that I saw for sale and he was beginning to consider home ownership. Think about it, rent was expensive. Even cheap rent would total four thousand dollars a year and two years of renting could cost you nearly ten thousand dollars. That was 20 % of the price of my home. In 10 years I would be living in a rent free home if I considered I had paid rent for 10 years.

Just like anywhere in the world the more popular a location the higher the price. Every book I read and every person I spoke with all said to wait a year before buying. Yea...like I had four thousand dollars to throw away while waiting for the right feeling to strike. Comparable houses outside of the central area were cheaper than houses near central but required a car or frequent bus or taxi commuting. The further out of *central* the more likely you were to find bigger lots. The bigger the lot and the better the view the more likely the price was going to be higher. The suburbs tended to have bigger lots and houses that were separated from each other by space and fences.

House prices, like rents, are likely to be half of what you might expect to pay for a similar home or apartment in *el Norte*. That varied from area to area and houses in San Jose might cost less than homes in Grecia. In comparison homes in Iowa or Tennessee might cost less than homes in Oregon, California or New York. A house, in an area that you might like, could cost as much per square foot as the house you are leaving in the States. Location, location, location.

I was not going to begin to try to wax pedantically about real estate choices. My only advice would be the same as always...go with your gut. It worked for me, but I was becoming pretty well practiced at listening to the inner voice. Practice increasing your sensitivity and you will be led to the right home for you.

CHAPTER 48, DAY 178, MIRACLES

Day 178, May Day, I went to the farmers market and some silly little shopping tricks crossed my mind. Oh yea... There were green onions sold both with the roots on and with the roots cut off. Green onions with the roots still on them are fresher and last longer in the fridge. Cilantro, on the other hand should have the roots cut off and be stood up in a cup of water as soon as possible before being stored in the fridge.

The eggs in the bags were the same eggs that were in the flats and they were all sold by weight in kilos. Rumor had it that the farmer's market eggs were better than the store eggs. If it mattered, someone would write a book about it.

I had so many stories in my head from just the last two days. I lost my rain coat, rain hat, pack, a bag of chips, and a candy bar in a plastic bag on a bus. Some guy friends from the hotel and I were making some local bus runs for *tourismo* (tourist) purposes and I hurried us all out the door without my gear. The next morning I flagged down that same bus only to reveal my bag of gear on the dashboard awaiting my arrival and retrieval.

That renewed my faith in person-kind on the heels of repeated plausible deniability by the airlines and TSA. The pilfered luggage items would not have been as valuable to me as the rain gear I left on the bus. I was blessed that God intervened and assisted me to abandon the baggage claim and returned to me what mattered most.

That same morning a fellow visiting the hotel told me the story of a Costa Rican drycleaner who returned a customer's license, credit card and three one hundred dollar bills. That same fellow who had that good fortune had just lost every personal belonging he owned when he went north for his mother's funeral. It seems the dog sitter backed a truck up to the door and took the furniture, appliances, et al. I thought he handled it very well. Maybe he handled it well because he had been in Costa Rica, off and on, for the last 18 years.

I also entertained an Austrian and his Taiwanese wife that were staying at the hotel across from the farmers market. They had been living in the US those forty years and resided in a half million dollar house, cum quarter million dollar home, in Reno Nevada. They were thrilled with Panama because of the reduced cost of consumer goods compared to Costa Rica. (I was originally headed to Panama but didn't have the funds to make residency.) It is true that some things are less expensive in Panama but some things are more expensive in Panama than in Costa Rica.

Under the new Costa Rican laws it was easier to complete residency requirements in Panama and it might even cost less to live there. Panama had higher medical standards and they used the US Dollar so there is no exchange rate to suffer. Maybe I would budget some money for a trip to Panama. I needed to make another visa renewal trip and Panama was somewhere I wanted to go.

Under the new rules for immigrating to Costa Rica I would encourage anyone wanting to expatriate to consider Panama. On my research spread sheet it ranked higher than Costa Rica as a preferred retirement spot. I just couldn't afford it. There were a couple of small towns in the Panamanian mountains that were reported to have altitude and climate conditions comparable to Grecia Costa Rica.

CHAPTER 49, DAY 181, SOCIAL LIFE

It is day 181 and I had yet to talk about a social life. Well, I hadn't one. Writing to friends was it. There were many single guys. There were many married couples. There were many small groups of friends...and then there were the *Ticos*. OK, I admit to having three or four male acquaintances that I visited regularly.

Jim was much more outgoing than I was and he had met quite a few *Gringos* down here. (I don't know how he broke into their clicks.) He said these guys had been here a long time and they all had the same lament. They were single and they could not find a suitable girl for a relationship. Admittedly some of those guys were not making any efforts to acculturate.

As for girls from the States; fa-git-a-bout-it. Jim was right about that one. Jim also said that unless you'd been here you could not appreciate what it was like to be here. Unless you had left your life in the States behind you could not appreciate what it was like to be truly on your own.

I could talk to gals from the States and they could listen to what I said about my life here. Unless they made that personal choice and committed themselves to the irreversible expatriate decision they would never understand my experience. I had a hard enough time just trying to put my experiences into words. I was never going to find the words that people living "the life" in *el Norte* could understand. Once I moved here I had to give up on women who lived there.

There was a dating site I started to look at for female companionship that had 280 Costa Rican female profiles. Those 280 profiles were for the entire country. The real kicker was that only about 30 of those profiles were active. Not one of those 30 gals lived in my town. For as far away as they lived they might as well have lived on the moon.

It seemed many *Tica* (not all mind you) are so scheming that they would marry just for the money. Yea, we all know that happens in the States too. But here are a couple stories… One guy I heard about took a trip back to the States and his wife had her brother come over and they took everything out of the house including the car. Another guy bought a house and car in his *Tica* girlfriend's name (titling property in Costa Rica could be complicated) and then she broke off the relationship and she kept "her" house and car.

I would not have to be married to have such bad luck befall me. In Costa Rica cohabitating for three years created a common law marriage with all the rights and privileges. Among those rights and privileges was divorce. Costa Rican courts leaned in the direction of the woman. If there was a dispute between a man and his wife, by law, the man must leave the house and the woman usually ended up with it. In summary, there are some reasons that the beautiful *Tica* were not as appealing as partners as they appeared at first glance. As for *Gringas*, I had not spoken with one who didn't want a handout, some free work or to be lavishly entertained.

I heard that prostitution and promiscuous sex was common here among the *Tica*, however, that was just sex. The northern concepts of intimacy were foreign here. They seemed to shun intimacy and attachment. *Ticos* seemed private and inaccessible. Most married women here did not wear wedding rings and infidelity was not viewed as a social problem.

By northern standards much of what happened in Costa Rica defied understanding. That could be why it was so hard to explain what happened here. Also, the more I acculturated the fewer commonalities I had with northern culture. It was not very *Tico* to describe *Tico* life. What's that expression? "Zen: don't even think about it." One cannot describe the indescribable.

CHAPTER 50, DAY 182, LOVE

It was day 182 and love was on my mind. I was thinking about Costa Rican love. No, not love for Costa Rica. I was considering the concept of Costa Rican style romantic love. I had said a few times that it was not like northern concepts of love with some judgment and feeling of superiority. I had written of manipulations and infidelity as if they were a bad thing. Looking closely at myself, I would say that I found the Costa Rican concepts of love tawdry and unacceptable.

I also remember writing: "Change, adapt or perish." Perhaps I should have considered my own advice. (Was it Steven Stills who wrote "If you can't be with the one you love, honey love the one you're with?") Moving here gave that old saw new meaning. Perhaps if I couldn't find the type of love relationship I liked, I could like the one I found. I was starting to step back from my northern fantasy of love and look at the Costa Rican concept of love in a new light.

Perhaps that non-possessive, non-demanding and unstructured approach to relationship was truly more loving than what passed for love in the US. I would have had to give up a bunch of expectations to have gone down that road. Northern love was starting to feel like a business deal. Perhaps those mutual expectations of northern love were more trouble and heartache than they were worth.

I don't remember if I wrote about my friend Sue from Oregon. I know I mentioned she gave me my first mosquito net, managed my money for me, wired funds and was an emergency contact. I had known Sue for almost 2 years. For a very brief period we were intimate and it was not the right path for us. We had remained close friends and she was a priceless asset in my moving process.

We had a mutual interest in hiking and weekend outings. Since none of our other friends were willing to spend their weekends exploring the great outdoors she and I spent a considerable amount of time together. We even talked on the phone regularly and knew the details of each other's lives. I thought we were very close friends and I loved her for the beautiful spirit that she possessed.

When I was going to go to Oregon for two weeks on business I was looking forward to seeing her and spending some time hiking. I also thought she would enjoy going to Roger's Easter potluck. Two weeks and a long list of things to do left me with little time to schedule for her. Before waiting to find out how it would all play out she was upset by my lack of attention and threatened to drop all my important documents at my buddy Roger's house and never see me again.

That little bit of personal history was meaningless. The meaningful part was that the northern women to whom I recalled the story thought she was in love with me. Was that what passed for love in the north? (Would I be willing to trade all that for a woman who might not show up when she said or who had sex with some other guy or stole my possessions if given the chance?) The trade off was, instead of throwing a fit, a *Tica* would most likely just fade into the sunset.

I lived in a jungle and life in the jungle was uncertain and impermanent. However, I was noticing that life up north was not much different than life down south. It was just that Hollywood had glossed over the reality of northern life and we only saw the façade of life. Take for example the belief that the US government was not corrupt and that the Latin governments were corrupt. The corruption in US government was so insipid and insidious you just couldn't see it. Things were more obviously flawed here and there was beauty in that. Costa Rican love was more obviously flawed and there was a beauty in that too.

CHAPTER 51, DAY 183, WHAT TO BRING

On day 183 three weeks had passed since my return from Oregon and I had accomplished some organizing and installing of my goods. I felt relief when hardware items were installed and working and I could see a few clear spots on the top of the desk. Both door sweeps were installed and I took the piece of tin out of the gap under the laundry door. I installed a laundry door automatic screen door latch to keep it closed and a cupboard handle to be able to pull the door into the latch. One of the solar lights worked and was now set on a motion detector to light the gate. Next to the light was a fake surveillance camera to fool any bad guys that might make it as far as the inner gate.

Despite all my efforts the solar shop light was not working. I would recommend solar devices for lighting here in Costa Rica as there was usually enough sun each day to power them. The five little walkway lights are providing free lighting. I thought that maybe the shop light had a factory defect. On my next trip I would buy more solar equipment and test it out before leaving town.

The weather center device with inside and outside temps, humidity and internal barometer was very useful at predicting the weather. I didn't have a good sense of the weather here and the electronics helped to clarify conditions. Funny enough it pretty consistently predicted fog when it was raining or about to rain.

Elsewhere in the electrical toys department the modem worked but I just choose not to use it, the notebook worked on the modem but needed formatting for the DSL, the photo cell light delay device was too tall for the light fixture, the answering machine now did everything it was supposed to do, the electrician specialty tools had already been useful and the tools and fasteners had been organized into containers and stowed.

That was just part of the 200 pounds of goodies I had brought with me. You would want to buy and bring all the electronic gadgets you might ever like to have because of the local process on electronics.

The closets and desks needed further attention. Sheets, blankets, towels, kitchen ware and clothes all needed homes. I was making order out of the books, legal papers, banking business and soft goods. The umbrella was a plus and the bandages had already come in handy. I brought a huge collection of adhesive bandages because the selection and availability were poor here. Might I also recommend an electric toothbrush with UV sanitizer? Maybe, I will type out the US shopping list for you.

This also was discount shopping day, and Jim had offered to take me out for brunch. There was no brunch here in Costa Rica Jim just ate breakfast near lunch time so he calls it brunch. Jim had borrowed some money from me until his ATM card arrived so he wanted to do something nice in return. He was the one who lost two ATM cards in two months and he had borrowed some money and had paid it back.

Every Thursday discount deals were available at the Roseville market. Everything was marked down on Thursday and the store was busy. Yesterday afternoon I stopped in the store for an impulse purchase and there were no shoppers to be seen. I guessed if people wanted something on Wednesday they just waited one more day for the discount.

The weird thing was that every check stand had a cashier on Wednesday and on many busy Thursdays only half the check stands were open. Latin living was about the *Gringo* accepting more than it was about the *Gringo* understanding. When looking for things to make sense I turned to my own personal world for solace and order. My thoughts and feelings might have been all over the chart but my physical world offered some logic and regime.

CHAPTER 52, DAY 187, *TICO* TIME

On 187 I felt I was becoming more *Tico*. I was *Tico* enough to say "*Tal vez.*" Maybe covered a multitude of sins. It was so typically *Tico* to offer to do something and to not do it. Four days ago I said I might write a copy of the shopping list the next day... Oh well?

I had been busy with yard work, and the hired help was good motivation to work really hard for three days. It was also nontraditional trash collection day in my barrio today. Well maybe... It was Costa Rica after all. Many bags filled with weeded out goose grass and pruned branches were outside the door awaiting pickup. The metal scroungers had been here and a neighbor asked for the broken sheet of clear plastic roofing. *Por su puesto* (Of course).

After 34 hours of work the overgrown mat and mess had been transformed into landscaping. Just like in my Fall Creek Oregon property there were plenty of ornamental native plants growing. We moved a major amount of dirt and double dug planting spots. With knowledgeable help it was possible to locate impatiens, coyote cilantro, red ginger, lantana, *minte*, datura arborea and four or more different *plantas bonitas* (pretty plants). Some of the plants looked like elephant ear and some begonia like leafy things. All the help, the finds in the yard, the potted plants and random events yielded a landscape composition of sorts.

Speaking of hired help and not doing what I said I would... A *Tica* story. The help, who was previously cameoed as "the house cleaner," was scheduled to show up at 7:00 A.M. Friday through Sunday. On Sunday, the day before trash pickup day, I called her cell phone at 8 AM and she told me to expect her at 9:00 AM and she showed up a little after 10:00 AM. (Time was a relative concept in Costa Rica.)

Those of you who recall the story of the maid and the missing cup might be asking yourself "Why?" Why would I hire an alleged pilferer? The answer was that it was good practice. I practiced my best security, my best manners, my best vigilance and my best psychic ability. Her work on Friday was all outside.

I had chairs outside and she somehow knew to leave her bag on the porch. Most of what was of value was hidden from view. I even took the bathroom table of toiletries out of sight from prying eyes. Things in the master bedroom of that were of use, value or that might be a temptation were hidden from view.

The guestroom shades were drawn and the door was closed. Nothing much of obvious value was visible anywhere. We seemed to be keeping it easy and simple and everything was closely supervised until some impulse seized her after about five or six hours of work. She suddenly stopped what she was doing and walked into the breezeway where her gear was and then proceeded to enter the screen door to the house. I followed her but before I reached the screen door she was coming out the house. Not a word was spoken.

This was what I meant by good practice. I thought I was pretty secure but she pointed out a weak spot in my preparations. Today, for the first time ever, she wanted to take a shower after working. Well, an empty room was an empty room. I had tried to theft-proof my house and I hoped I would develop habits and practices that helped others to avoid temptation.

I learned how to make the *Entrada sin permiso* (entrance without permission) stop. It was simple to stop her from just walking into the house. I only needed to keep the door locked and the key in my pocket. No one spoke a word about it. I used a smaller shampoo bottle in the shower. I covered the cabinets in the kitchen with fabric to hide the cooking gear. I might be considered rich by some warped perspective but it was essential that I not appear rich.

CHAPTER 53, DAY 190, BOTANICAL GARDENS

On day 190 I went to Sarchie with Jim. I had been on four little adventures with Jim and did not know how true it was that I would be willing to make unlikely friends. Eventually I want what I want and I will do without rather than have less than I want. The chain smoking was one thing but throwing cigarette butts in a urinal was a whole new level of disgust! And then there was the waiting.

We all need some excuse for friends no matter what the cost. Even having *Tico* friends required putting up with a bunch of time related weirdness. (Life here often seemed strange compared to life in the US.)

Jim did not schedule anything. It was all luck of the draw with him and he had been very lucky. Even if I was at his place at 9 AM never left before 11:00 AM. I figured I could save myself an hour or two of waiting for Jim by showing up at 11. I still had to wait... And we left at 12:30 to take an hour trip to a place that closed at four o'clock. Then he complained that we did not have enough time in the gardens. He also complained about the heat of the day but he would not go outside until nearly midday.

I usually woke early in the morning and by noon I had already been on my feet for six or seven hours. The one hour of rest while traveling in the heat of the day was not enough to prepare me for the hills of the *Jardin Botanico* (Botanical Garden). It was spectacular. From the office I could see a maze formed by hibiscus that must be most amazing in full bloom. At the park we picked up maps in English and German, and walked through the palm garden. We stood near the maze at about 2:30 and there was no shade so I did not stroll around the maze. What took us so long to reach the gardens was Jim's need for a beer run and then trying to find ice for the warm beer.

The palm garden, wow, wow, wow; followed by a heliconia garden that was even more wow, wow, wow. I want, I want, I want. Sooo much cool stuff. Pictures? I took many of them. Then, there are the bromeliaceae gardens and they too made for many great photo opportunities. I had set up and taken a good number of shots but I had neglected to check for the SD card. The SD card was out for downloads and all my picture taking was for not. If you want pictures… go to www.elsegarden.com.

I did take notes and had my garden book and I will certainly plan a trip with a sketch pad, a camera with an SD card, extra batteries and a wealth of time. The two hours Jim and I spent was on less than half the gardens. There were forests, fruit trees, water gardens, cactus and flower gardens to see. There had to be six hours of adventure here if you planed to take pictures and notes. The gardens were like a cross between a southern mansion, Disneyland and an Oregon style interpretive trail. It was also bigger and older than I imagined. There were plants the shape and size of which I had never seen before. The flowers looked like they were sketched to be illustrations for *Alice in Wonderland*.

Down the rabbit hole I fell and each layer of descent was more extreme than the last. All that wonder came crashing back to reality when we reached the orchid garden which was not in bloom. The orchid garden's saving grace was that it identified perennially blooming orchid. We had a short romp through the cactus which looked very common except for the thorn free variety that is a commonly spinney breed.

I found that my preferences were toward plants from Peru and Bolivia. I enjoyed seeing much of it but I was ready to leave. I felt evening coming on. The office was closed at 4:30 and as luck had it a guy locking up offered to call a taxi for us. Again Jim had the luck of the draw. Drunks must have their own very special patron saints for that kind of thing to happen to him so regularly.

CHAPTER 54, DAY 192, *GRINGO* FANTASY

On day 192 I belonged in a Zoo. I was experiencing another day of wonder. I could brag about the great park and send pictures. You should have been there. [I know some of you still harbor fantasies of some paradise with semi-nude tropical ladies serving up Pina Colatas to the *Gringos* as they lounge around. You forgot to mention these gals all speak perfect English and the drinks are *gratis* (free). Get a grip.] Other than not speaking the language what could ever worry a person on a diminishing income living on foreign soil? No matter what I wrote, some readers still had some wild notions about what it was like to live in Costa Rica. I have included a chat I just had with my cousin.

SHE: No, the dating game. I would have thought dating would have been one of the easiest things.

ME: Don't feel bad about not knowing what it was like here. Most people have some fantasy. You should hear some of the comments I have heard. For example: "I would sit in the sun all day long."

Did you think all Costa Rican women spoke English and were *Gringo* crazy? They barely spoke fluent Spanish and just like anywhere else in the world they had disdain for outsiders. Everything was the same all over the world. You didn't see a bunch of White women chasing after the non-English speaking guys who migrate to New Jersey did you?

SHE: I really did think that the Costa Rican women would just love to be with a *Gringo*. I really was learning from your missives that being a tourist and living there are really two quite different realities. When we've traveled to many of the islands, people had been exceptionally friendly which, after reading what you've written, is probably just because we are the tourists. Do you think much of the thievery and suspicion is because of the falsehood that all Americans are very wealthy?

ME: The day the cleaning lady stole two cups from my cupboard her last comment at the gate was, "You're rich." That was a justification for sure but they steal from each other too. The main justification was "I want/need this." In Costa Rica confrontation was unacceptable so you were not supposed to say anything. Also, they are distant and suspicious of each other and though outwardly very friendly they keep very private. The more someone wanted from me, and the more they thought they could obtain something from me the friendlier they were. If I was not be an easy mark they turned the charm off, and it was as if I did not exist, or worse.

OK, the cousin diary; what was the point of that? Oh yea, I belong in a zoo. No one ever really imagined the things that made Costa Rica so wonderful. That morning I saw a clear butterfly lighting and flying against the fixed pane of a window. It wanted out and eventually crossed over to the open part. In the meantime I could see through its wings to the leaves on the trees outside the window, through the wings!

That didn't happen every day but that was a much more realistic fantasy of Costa Rican life than most of the things that come out of the mouths of *Gringos* here and abroad. Once there was a fire fly in the yard intermittently lighting a spark. Amazing to have watched the tracers and gauge his flight. Eventually he crossed the yard and I could not believe he landed on me. It was too bad I involuntarily jerked my arm away in surprise.

All of a sudden the computer service has become very sketchy. Perhaps it was the impending weather. There were low clouds with rolling thunder in the distance, flashes of light on the horizon and threatening drops of rain. Tomorrow *Invierno* (winter) officially begins. I had accomplished an incredible amount of excavating, moving plants, preparing soil, picking rocks, pulling weeds, locating utility pipes and there was still more to be done before the rains really hit hard.

CHAPTER 55, DAY 196, WEATHER

Day 196 and Oh Wow!! Weather! I loved weather. It was the great outdoors/gardener part of me...the old farmer gene sprouting forth. That day was beyond describable. The clouds were what I would have expected to see at five to seven thousand feet. They were so close I felt like I could touch their thunderous majesty. Oh Wow!!

There were great cracks of lightening followed by rolling roars. It cracked, boomed and banged around. I looked up to see where it was happening from the sound of it. It was right overhead a bird's flight from me. It felt like such a grand event I would look to see where the racket was being made and there was nothing. There were only billowing white/gray clouds sliding by seamlessly as if the thunder never existed.

I heard thunder that sounded like a string of firecrackers going off. I heard great metal doors slamming closed at the ends of deep tunnels. There was the crack of a falling oak followed by the blue angels roaring by just over the grandstands. That show came to town almost every afternoon accompanied by the ring of rain on metal roofs punctuated by the rhythmic dull drip of the leak into the bucket.

It was somewhere near 76 degrees and the humidity was in the 60's. The weather center 24 hour forecast was for rain that afternoon and it did rain. It pelted down cold rain at first and soon it was throwing it down in buckets. Inside temperatures were still high because the building was warm.

I put on my bloody-well look-alike for an Australian cork hat (without the corks) and admired the landscaping work. (The hat had been repeatedly treated with Sno Seal and coats of silicone spray and worked great that time.) I had a new drainage ditch as of that morning and access to the pipe that leads to the street. Everything seemed to be doing admirably in that early light rain.

That was not the rain I remembered of the tropical afternoons on Saint John Island. On St. John walking in the afternoon rain was comfortable and cooling. Here it was chilling. It might have been in the 70's but it felt like it was in the 50's. Eventually the rain warmed and the drain continued to drain and I was really enjoying walking around in my hat, flip/flops and soaking wet shorts and Hawaiian shirt. But I was not here to be a weather forecaster. I was here to write about the expatriate experience. Yet it was the yard work that gave me focus and sanity.

Without the household projects my life might just fall off the face of the earth. Everything was now on auto pilot and I had many established rituals and routines. These ceremonies gave me clear purpose and inspiration. I was focused on planning a garden and shopping for plant ideas. The writing was good but I had been remiss about making time to edit.

I went back to the town of Sarchie and revisited the Botanical Gardens to shoot a bunch of photos and make notes on plants of interest and revisited the world's largest oxcart. Everything in the gardens had changed in just a short time. Well, it was fall.

CHAPTER 56, DAY 201, RETIREMENT

On day 201 I was back at work in the yard. I had heard many times that retirement could consume a lot of time. With structured work the tendency was to ignore certain projects. Certain jobs were delayed or farmed out to others. The money I made working went to pay someone else to do what I needed done.

Lack of sustained income and an unknown future created a sense of necessity. I was the only one who would look out for my needs. I brought myself with me and had replicated my US experience by adopting aspects of the culture that fit my personality. I liked to work. I was industrious and able. So I was a busy guy with absolutely nothing I had to do. Was there really nothing to do? Maybe, if I stayed at a hotel, let the maids clean and do laundry and ate my meals out daily there would be nothing to do.

The burst of yard work helped put my more daily needs in perspective. I needed to wash the dirty work clothes. I needed to buy and cook food. I needed to clean the kitchen and the house in general. Having help seemed to create more work. There was cooking food to feed the helper and subsequent kitchen cleaning and then cleaning the tools and putting them away and policing the work area in general. Add some obsessive reading to that and I was a busy man.

I had a couple of regular chore days. Thursday and Saturday were big shopping days and sometimes involved finding someone to watch my purchases while I shopped for more and then bused it home. Sunday had defaulted to laundry/housecleaning day. Squeeze some morning yard work in there and I had pretty full weeks of activity. Friday I took a hazy day off to sit in the gray and read. Just a few hours in the gray and I was sunburned. I was surprised and happy I only pinked out and did not really hurt myself.

I guessed I needed to schedule in downtime too. There were so many little attention getters that could take forever to resolve. I just couldn't seem to attend everything. For those of you who want to make a to-do list for yourself I might suggest: you obtain a Costa Rican driver's license; check on *Caja* (the government health plan; find someone to help access and translate the use of *Banco National* online; closely monitor US based accounts, bills and reservations; determine if an attorney can complete the transfers of utilities; struggle with changing the name on the utility bills; provide *Apartado* address to DSL and the utility providers so they don't just throw the statement letter over the wall as a form of postal delivery; cancel Verizon phone in the US if the internet ever comes back online and look into changing the DSL account to auto-pay from the dollars account to avoid paying the exchange rate. Then, I might try saying all that in one breath! Monday was usually a busy day in town and would be a good day for a day off.

Having more than one scheduled activity accomplished in a day was considered a small miracle here. So, picking up some drain parts from the *ferreteria* (hardware store) was an all day event. If I were lucky I would even get them installed in the same day. As with the summer sun, the winter rain also affected scheduling. It rained until 6:30 that morning and that was new and could lengthen. Usually I worked on the same schedule winter and summer; I worked outside in the morning and in the afternoon I went inside and hid or sat under cover and watched the weather.

I had been insane for ten days as I had committed myself and my finances to the yard work? I did yard work of all kinds: planning, planting, preparing future projects and locating and creating utility channels. I gauged the profundity of my gardening experience by how many of my marbles I found. Though I had not realized that I had lost my marbles in the first place, if found, they must have been lost at one time. (Those of you who garden at older home sites know what I mean.) Three of my marbles reappeared during this gardening project; two of the glass ones and one of my favorite opaque marbles. (How come I never find any of the shooters or cat's eyes?)

Nevertheless I was busy; as busy as I needed to be. The house and the yard work gave me focus and gobbled up all of my time and my budget money. It seems that the lifestyle I left behind was the lifestyle I brought with me. My life, in some very fundamental way, had not changed a bit. I still experienced all the same joys, challenges and idiosyncratic quirks that I had in the US. Everything in my life had been the same but I was living in a different place. Living in a different place made everything seem different even if it was all the same.

CHAPTER 57, DAY 202, FEELING GRAY

Day 202 and the gray in the sky and the sudden slowing of activity had me feeling alone in the world. I preferred distractions that seemed to lead to a future. I preferred to look forward rather than to look within at myself. In my most bored and alone times I found that I still wanted to do something. That something was usually attached to an outcome at some later time.

I must have felt lonely because I wrote two days in a row. Funny what I had learned about myself by just paying attention. This was my week number five of the six week cycle of adjustment. It seemed to me that the writing created the fantasy of a future or some illusion that what was being done today would have an outcome in some vague unforeseeable future. Gosh it sounded like finding religion.

I was guessing that even expats with partners felt that same isolation. A single relationship could not fill your life but there would still always be that foreign feeling. The feeling of superficiality in local relationships was much more obvious here than in the US

Moving here was reminiscent of my experience in changing jobs. Once I was no longer in the common bond of employment the connection with co-workers started to weaken and eventually the friends from work were lost entirely. So it was when I left the country. My connections with my *Gringo* friends started to be strained by the distance and the less personal modes of communication. I did not know too many people who liked to send emails. And spending time on the phone seemed to be a challenge.

People want to hang out with people. That is what people do, we flock together. We don't call and we don't write; we visit. I needed to spend more time developing local contacts. My question was, "With whom?"

Do I look for my friends in the old friends that I had left in the states? With the curious people in the States whom I had never met? With my paid *Tico* help? With the *Gringos* with whom I could not expect to find a common bond? With online friends that I was likely to never meet and who were just as likely to vanish from the face of the earth?

What would it have been like to see/contact no one for a day or two? I mean no shopping, walking in town, local calls, internet email not even sitting down to write something to an imaginary someone. I could have had my own little Zen retreat right here in *lote* 31.

It was odd how I filled my time and what drew my attention. I was not sure how my priorities were formed anymore. Yes, protection from the weather and my desire to eat were still high on the priority list. How would I meet my social needs? Life was grand and I am in heaven. Maybe another time I would Zen out. Right now I had to figure out how to go online to the bank to see if they made the phone and internet auto-pays because I did not receive my notice by email. It was probably OK because the phone and electricity were still working. Ha ha ha. In any case, I wanted to keep tract of the account withdrawals.

I prioritized by the size of the blaze. I extinguished the biggest fire first and just hoped for the best. There were more loose ends than would be tied in the next six months. Someone once told me that things calmed down after the first year. I hoped this was true. I saw no end to the little details that made my move feel so complicated and complex.

CHAPTER 58, DAY 205, GARDENING AND COOKING

On day 205 there seemed to be more birds in the air (or I never saw them winging?) and indeed the four or five little baby birds that were in the nest outside my window were awing and away. Yesterday I took a trip to three nurseries. About five dollars in travel money for two and the balance of fifteen dollars spent on guidance, opinion and entertainment. There had been two delightfully sunny days as the temperatures were in the 70's and spring-like conditions existed.

The *Jardin Botanico* was one thing. A plant book was another. Then, there was what was available to purchase at retail outlets. I continued to plan a garden... Life could be so hard. LOL. However, there had been two days of sunshine and with the sunshine came two days of earthquakes. Nothing was crashing to the ground but the ground was gently swaying and just not as you think it should be.

I was beginning to understand the ground effect and I hoped I could describe it before it made me too rattled to put it into words. The ground shook in the nurseries as I found few of the plants that were in the *El Jardin Botanico* and the common plant field guide. They were growing plants to sell not to replicate nature. Many plants I could find free for the taking if I knew where to look.

After two hours in the first nursery the cleaning lady and I walked uphill to check out a few more nurseries. The air was perfect. The houses were well kept. The grounds were spacious and lavishly planted and I asked myself; "Self," I asked "Why didn't it dawn on me that the best area in which to live was going to be where the nurseries were?" These business locations were run by people whose livelihoods depended on good weather.

It would take longer than the seven hours I spent on the adventure to describe it. Nurseries varied greatly in their preparedness and retail approach; some were weedy and overgrown and others were slick and polished.

The day 206 adventure was going to be even more difficult to describe. It started with shopping for cheese, fruit and veggies: $12. The cost for the help buying and preparing seven *Tico* dishes: $10. Having family for a morning: priceless!

It started as a simple work assignment: Go to the *Feria* (Farmers' market) and buy all the strange and exotic fruits and veggies I could find and prepare them. With the help of Flor, the maid, cum landscaper, cum culinary guide I had two big bags of grocery items. That process involved: walking around the farmer's booths guessing who had the best price, pointing out items that I did not recognize and asking *Te gusta?* (You like?). I then had to interpret the response and ask *Mas o menos?* (More or less) Should I buy or not?

The twenty minute walk up over the hill and down to my *barrio* with the groceries had me wishing we had taken the local bus and I was calculating the cost of a taxi versus paying Flor by the hour to walk. Well, I had nothing but time and it cost half as much to walk as it did to pay the cab fare. I was also curious as to how Jimina, Flor's daughter, was going to hold out in her new sandals.

I had neglected to tell you that Flor showed up for work with an 8-year-old daughter in tow. Throughout the market we were also on a shoe hunt for the little munchkin who was giving me the shy silent treatment. As uninterested in interacting as she appeared, Jimina did not interfere with the shopping process. Jimina did have beautiful flowing hair. What would you expect from the daughter of a hairdresser?

Now that I had that kid in my house what is a guy going to do? Break out the tools so she could build something? Put her to work at the kitchen counter over which she could barely see? Give her a machete and let her loose in the garden? Did she bring a game boy? Thank God for colored pencils. That and the back of 46 pages of a hard copy draft of the book (used for editing during air travel) were available as drawing paper.

Saved! After drawing some pictures she wanted to engage in a version of button-button, except hiding a folded piece of art work she had drawn in the front room. All that time food was being prepared in the kitchen. I did my best to describe the seven dishes we (prepared:

There was a spice ball that was cut in half and mashed into a pot of water with a little sugar; that made a jar full of a slightly tart *tamarindo* drink. A watered down version of that goes a long way, even though it might be high in vitamin C. Then, *ensalada* was made from a beet like root that does not taste like a US beet. Cleaned, peeled, and grated the beet and carrot were tossed with cubed cucumber and the juice from a small lemon. Also, on the table was *plantano*. Flor was quite taken aback by the absence of *plantano* in the American diet. That might be the original fried banana. If you've not had fried banana at home you should try it. *Plantano* (it only looks like an oversized banana) was plantain fried in oil and was usually added to rice or other dishes. I just ate them. They were more fibrous and starchy than a banana but greasy and better in small doses.

Another table had four dishes on it and the things that looked like big acorns were *Pejibaye* and they are sold hot, ready to peel, cut in half and stuff with tuna and mayo. It was a starchy fruit. I would say it had a neutral or maybe nutty taste and a soft root like texture. The big green on the outside vegetable that looked like pumpkin was boiled into a spaghetti squash consistency with a sweet potato taste. Then we had two mixed vegetable plates. First we had a mash of *camote* and *nompi* flavored with butter and a sprinkling of salt. That equated to having a mashed potato and a sweet potato combo. This was made from hairy dirty balls and a pinkish root. Everything was boiled until soft and peeled and mashed. For the entre we had diced *ayote* and *chayote* boiled to perfection and garnished with a chicken *chorizo* and flavored with a cube of bullion. These were summer squash and they had pear and gourd like appearances respectively.

Before the cooking was completed the girls were all of a sudden at the gate looking up the hill. I was in the kitchen and stopped to discover what the event was; we were also having 11-year-old boy company. So, there arrived a boy, a back pack, and a bunch of bicycle parts. Now, we were all speaking Spanish but only some of us understood what was being said and it wasn't me. The happy four of us gathered around the kitchen counter and ate *bocas* (appetizers) and caught up on the morning's activities. I was literally laughing out loud at the scene.

OK, let's not forget the fruit plates. You probably all know papaya; it was peeled, gutted and cut into strips. It made a great shake and was easy to eat. We also had a buttery avocado mashed into a guacamole that I was still not sure was *major* (better) than the Hass type that was also available here. The *Guyaba* looked like a green apple and had all the flavor of a green apple but better in some way. You could buy Washington apples in the stands, but *Guyaba* was fresher wetter and had not much of a core (the smaller seeds were more scattered in the meat); just wash, cut and eat.

Then I had a refrigerator full of food, a new selection of veggies and fruits, a little set of local recipes and some refrigerator art. After the hide and seek of the "secret art" three drawings were left for me. I had myself as the white rabbit. I had colored orange slice shapes, *y me favorito* (and my favorite), there was me as the center of a flower on which each of the petals had a letter and a heart on it.

Now, there was the beauty from my old fart perspective... I paid them and off they went. Rent a family. I think it could work?! Maybe? It was totally cool for me. Kids always required a special kind of attention and I was glad the visit was short and I was very happy for the experience. I felt richer if not more exhausted for their visit. I would have liked to have felt honored by the experience but it was just typical *Tico*. There were no clear boundaries on anything in Costa Rica and what boundaries that did exist seemed to move around excessively. Separation of family and work was part of the cultural difference between *el Norte* and Costa Rica. People bring their kids to workplaces here and the kids are well mannered and courteous. This was better than if we were real family I imagined.

CHAPTER 59, DAY 212, EARTHQUAKES

It was day 212 and I was hard pressed to believe I had been here seven months. It was a frigid 67 degrees and I had goose bumps. Last night when it hit 70 I was looking for a shirt and laughing to myself in a Boris Karloff/Jim Carey kind of way. It was baffling how what once seemed comfy and warm had turned nippy. I woke early to the sound of the trash truck and as soon as I had relieved myself I jumped right back into bed. I was freezing at what was probably 63 degrees.

I had grown accustomed to those 70 degree mornings and had found them comfortably cool. Like at the hotel, I hung out at home with little on and donned my long pants, shoes, shirt and hat before heading to town. By the time I returned from town I was usually burning up but I was not sunburned. Odd that standing in the snowy weather just seven weeks prior to this did not seem bitter cold.

I was a little under the weather and maybe I was being more temperature sensitive than usual. Perhaps 65degrees was not really that cold. But I felt the pressure front change. My ears popped as if I were driving up or down a mountain. Though it was 78 degrees I felt a chill in the air and within a half hour it was 73 degrees F. and dropping. Life seemed to change dramatically in Costa Rica. Maybe the weather was all the instruction in drama and hypersensitivity necessary for a whole culture of people?

I was less prone to write when I felt ill. And today I was on day five of a nasty head cold. A local friend, Carlos, recently had the same infirmity. I had a bad runny nose, resultant chest congestion, followed by persistent cough. That would all stop in a total of seven to fourteen days but in the meantime it was a dampener. I was retired and I had nothing better to do with my time other than lay around and recuperate.

However, I was dying to write, work in the yard or even clean house. I decided that it was a good time to do research on the *sacudidos* (earthquakes). Attempting to restrain myself from strenuous effort I limited my yard work and house work and trips to *central* (the town center) and concentrated my efforts to lying still. Believe me when I tell you that lying still was hard work.

If you try it for a while you will agree. This lying around furthered my research into the effect of constant earth movement upon psychological development. After just a short time of opening myself up to the deeper feelings I was having during the events (which were close to constant) I caught a glimpse of the insecurities established in the Costa Rican genetic memory. Just imagine what it would be like if your entire life was spent walking, running, riding and driving on wet ice.

The result would be that we would still learn to run, skip and jump and life would continue and prosper but you could never really trust your footing. We might not rely on being able to do something a second time because the opportunity might literally slip away. As I laid there I felt the liquid nature of the earth below me and pondered the psychological consequences (it was more like the earth moving continually rather than a shaking or quake). I had read about cultural personality traits and this seemed to explain their origin.

It did not leave me feeling very trusting (grounded if you will) and maybe it even made me a bit edgy and suspicious of anything that might appear reliable. Many researchers had documented the behaviors but not the cause. Other *Gringos* had even noticed them. I had gathered anecdotal evidence that supported the theorems but no one had explained why they are that way. I postulated that it was a history of environmental factors that had created the Costa Rican personality type.

Maintaining focus was difficult when it seemed that anything you focused upon changed or was eaten quickly. That might be the reason it felt like a country of drunks. The physical environment affected us all and the effect was intoxicating. I was sucked into the vortex myself and I hoped to keep my wits about me.

CHAPTER 60, DAY 215, *TICO* PERSONALITY

Day 215 had me preoccupied with so many little to do's. I was writing. I was still unsure what drove me here but here I was. I thought that writing openly and frequently changed the way I thought somewhat. It seemed difficult to distinguish between culturally related changes and changes due to other factors.

The sun was shining that morning. I wondered if I should strip the bed and start washing sheets. Minimally I had to put yesterdays wash back out on the clothesline to finish drying. Someday I will devote a page to doing laundry *Tico* style. Just buy: silk, rayon, linen and microfiber and life will be much easier.

It was the *Ticos* and the adaptation process that I wanted to write about today. I was becoming more open because I was actually becoming more closed. I was becoming *Tico* friendly, outgoing, gratuitous, rhetorical, superficial and ego-centered. I wrote a tremendous amount and that gave me less to talk about. I had an outlet to express my doubts, fears and concerns. Writing gave me a bench on which to work the tools of life and straighten whatever might be bent. It was somewhat like dreaming out loud. Until that moment I had never believed journaling possessed any therapeutic value. Maybe writing openly and sharing what was written had more value than hidden prose.

I was sharing the observations and the stories I had heard from others and the generalizations I that had sprung from both. Just like all generalizations, I could not apply these stereotypes to all *Ticos* and I like to think that I am not a stereotypical American.

Maybe I did not need deep friends because my depth was exhausted on paper, or was it due to the bombardment of inconsistency that I was becoming more reticent. People had written that *Ticos* were outwardly open and inviting while being private and modest. I called that behavior repressed. I was new here, but I had heard the same stories from the old-time ex-pats and the locals alike. *Ticos* would not let you into their lives in a West-coast American way. However, they would be happy to literally move themselves into your life.

This socially sanctioned lack of boundaries made it easy to understand *Tico* privacy. If people wanted to push themselves into my life and take things as if they were their own, and if the moral code supported that behavior, then I had better be pretty private with my life and my possessions.

Ticos also had to be the world's worst liars. There was always a huge tell when they lied. The story was too big or way too different from what they had said beforehand. Sometimes it was nonchalant and other times their face was riddled with guilt. Even the good guys who would never steal from me would support any lie if it would help a situation appear smoother. They seemed not to care that the deception was obvious.

I was not making assumptions and I had more stories to support these comments and no room to write testimonies for each. Believe me when I say it was Latin living in a rainstorm deception. (Most of you could rightfully say "I would not want to live that way"). So, I just wear a rain coat, or carry an umbrella.

A *Gringo* I knew had been here for over a year and he said his friends had told him he seemed changed from the person they had known in the States. If I was following the conversation correctly he was referring to his becoming more closed, distant and self-centered. That reminded me of a whole new class of *Gringo* I realized existed. There were people who lived here with some sense of permanence and there were people who lived out of one suitcase. There was an entire class of single suitcase *Gringos* here who liked being foot loose and free to run at any time.

CHAPTER 61, DAY 217, HOME IMPROVEMENT

It was day 217 of This Old House. The jungle seemed to be more interested in consuming the house than did the rain. My previous efforts and concentration had been on rain proofing the place. This was a job which lingered on to the inevitable punch list. (For those of you not in the trades, a punch list is the list of: flaws, corrections needed and errors and mistakes to be corrected. Usually the buyer provided the list to the installer who thought he was at the end of his job.) That is a long winded way of saying there was a leak here and there. There were a couple of loose or over tightened screws that needed attention and an intermittent torrent in the breezeway. I couldn't determine if the leaks were caused by the wind blowing the rain sideways? Was it creeping in under some overlap? Perhaps it was?

Even with global warming those who retired in tropical climates had to deal with rain. One long timer told me "Every house leaks. You just put a pan under it and wait for it to stop." It was difficult to determine intermittent water leaks. I think you had to be blessed with the ability to divine water to be able to track leaks. Some folks could do it.

I was fortunate that it was a dry year. Unfortunately the country was in the world market of agribusiness. The drying trend was hurting the coffee business and global economic frustration was negatively affecting the sugar market. I was watching inflation spiral here just like it was in the US. And the prices at restaurants and the cost of packaged coffee seemed to be climbing quickly.

How did that effect my being lazy about home repair? It did not affect it at all. It did affect the costs for my projects that were yet to be completed. Labor and building supply prices usually followed the increases in food costs.

I needed to keep the jungle from eating the back of the house and I needed to keep it from coming into the laundry room windows. I imagined that in the past permission was granted by the neighbor to pass through their house for trimming the tree behind the house or they hung out the window with the machete and wacked away at the jungle.

In back of the house was a slope dropping down to a river that was my backyard so to speak. Many neighbors had fruit trees, compost heaps, clothes lines and junk piles off the backs of their houses. My house had a tall block wall facing the area and it was also becoming part of the jungle as plants were taking root inside the wall. Individual access was necessary to use, maintain and/or improve the area. Other than just controlling the growth behind the house there was also potential for expansion into the area. I did not want to bother the neighbor...

Just like buying furniture, the passage to out back was something for which to budget. The landscaping was a *pasatiempo* (pastime). And I needed to maintain the yard, which I would have liked to have hired out for six dollars a week. All I needed was just a few hours of weeding a week to keep things under control. I still found money for improvements but I wanted to work the local plant collections angle first. I dreamed of a larger construction project in the front of the house but I had budgetary constraints. I could not be lulled into the feeling that everything was affordable even if it was cheaper than I was accustom to paying.

Moving here was like going to a winter gear closeout sale. There were great prices on the gloves, coats, hats and tents. These items that I could do without were at bargain prices. Everything was cheap by comparison to US prices but that did not mean I could afford it. It was monopoly money thinking; as if the money, because it was not dollars, was not real.

My dream projects were to redo the front wall and sidewalk, and to build a balcony to give myself a sunset view. That project amounts to a garden house with a stout roof and stairs on the outside. Just like my home in Cottage Grove Oregon I just couldn't leave well enough alone. There was always another mountain to climb and it was all about the climb. Providence would take its' course. Maybe the garden room was in a ten-year plan or maybe plans would change.

Gardening seems to be about change and garden plans seemed to have a life of their own. My gardens in Oregon had seemed to conform to the broad strokes but the details changes constantly. It seemed that the only thing that was constant was that things changed.

CHAPTER 62, DAY 220, SECURITY

Day 220 of *Tico* living or, was it possible to live with the *Tico*? I kept hearing about the greater trustworthiness of Nicaraguan and Panamanian people. I thought I could keep my *Tico* life separate from my personal life and survive with my possessions and privacy intact.

Yesterday I had an interesting conversation with a *Gringo*. I was finding there were many kinds of *Gringos* to meet. There seemed to be an abundance of single suitcase *Gringos*. That *Gringo* rented and either had a small income, or none, and had no ties to the community or country. The no-income *Gringos* worked at whatever illegal scams they could. I said illegal because a *Gringo* without permanent residence, or a work visa, cannot legally earn money in the country.

There were also the trust-fund types. They had money from family and even though they might have worked on occasion they never needed to earn a living. They were here for the easy living. Well, it was one of these trust-funders that I met yesterday and he had been living in Costa Rica for 18 years. He was the person I mentioned before who had the three $100 bills returned by the drycleaner and it was his house that was completely emptied by his dog sitter while he was at his mother's funeral in Florida.

This trust-fund fellow said that even though the Costa Ricans will bad rap the Nicaraguans, the Nicaraguans were more trusting and trustworthy. Being more trustworthy compared to not at all trustworthy was a small improvement. He said that he first tried to theft-proof his life and kept things simple and secure. I was building my life into one lockable room. Anything that was important to me or of monetary value was either in that room or behind a door or curtain.

He said he did all that security stuff and it was still wearing on him. The psychological weight of constantly being guarded took a toll over time. It didn't mean I couldn't have toys. It just meant I needed to keep my toys locked away and take them out to use them and then put them away again. At first I had a big cabinet in the bathroom full of t-shirts, towels, socks and sundries. My painter guy started poking around in the cabinet when he used the bathroom. He started helping himself to my US imported antacids. I tried to bring a five-year supply of everything I thought I might need ha ha.

Now cabinet needed to go to the locked room and a small table with sea shells, a candle, tooth brush and sundry items was there instead. I soon began to worry about losing the small collection of shells left by the previous owner. I thought that I would not want little trinkets walking away. They too had to go to the locked room and even the table of toiletries was moved to a bedroom to be away from prying eyes. I was building a little shop in the locked room that would hold my tools and gave me a small work space that was easily covered. I built a drill index and tool and bit stand on a 15 inch piece of one by six inch wood.

Now, for the lesson in humility that only living Latin could offer: I cannot show anyone my magnificent drill index and tool and bit stand. First of all, it would just be showing off which was frowned upon by *Ticos*. Then, it would be having more than the other guy and lastly it invites theft. The story goes that the friend doesn't steal from you, he just mentions what you have to someone else and it was that other person who stole it.

I felt very safe in the house and did not think I had to worry about burglary. However, having a very Spartan and Zen like public appearance would not hurt. I always had the internet to brag on...none of my internet friends knew where I lived, so I didn't have to worry about them grabbing my stuff. Ha ha ha...

CHAPTER 63, DAY 221, BEING A FOREIGNER

On day 221 I felt Lost and Alone. Hey, two movie titles combined. Speaking of movie titles, I kept thinking about that movie with Tom Hanks where he worked for a Fed Ex-like place and the plane went down. He was stranded on an island. An assortment of packages and indigenous materials were at hand. He made a friend of Wilson, the soccer ball, and almost goes mad from isolation, despair, disillusion, disappointment and whatever a person might feel in that situation.

It could be hard to sort out the exact feelings. It could be difficult to distinguish between loss, disappointment, jealousy and envy. "I wish I had what I don't have" and "I wish I had what they have" are not very far apart in a selection of words or thoughts. So…what was I feeling?

I believe our modern day Robinson Crusoe held out for hope of a future based on his experience of the past. That turned out to be illusion in the end. No expectations; no disappointments. He still had hopes. His unfulfilled plan for a future was what helped him through the desperate moments of his solitude.

So: Be happy, don't worry. Stay in the moment and find bliss in that existence. There was bliss in every moment. *Paz* (Peace) was at hand. I loved my letter reading audience of 13, my Wilson, if you will. They too will be sorely missed when finally we drift apart. Then I will truly be adrift and alone in a sea of confusion. The writing gave me focus and future all in one.

How unholy of me to be having a human experience. I offer the would-be traveler or expatriate no advice on the topic of finding peace which meant that this was something I finally understood. I understood that I did not understand the deeper workings of the psyche, the mind or the human spirit. The more I knew, the more I knew I didn't know.

That was something else about moving to a foreign land. When I thought I understood something I would discover that I was looking at life from a Northern perspective. This was not the native perspective. I might have observed something in the local behaviors. I might have learned some coping skills. But, that was entirely different than internalizing the cultural concepts.

What threw me the most was the lack of conceptualization. For example, did you know that Native Americans had no word for or concept of a wheel when the Europeans arrived? It must have baffled the colonists who tried to describe the concept (which they took for granted) to the indigenous people. The locals probably smiled and nodded as *Gringos* used words and hand gestures in their search for a pre-made wheel.

I could see that the Costa Ricans did not share the northern concept of love. They also did not share our northern concept of regularity. Time was relative. Fine…you think you are going to teach the Costa Rican to become *Gringo*… So I would hope. This is the point where the astute among you are laughing out loud.

This teaching other cultures the American-way was the most common *Gringo* misunderstanding of the expatriate experience. I can't relax for a minute in the polluted pools of my northern cultural experience. I was thinking all wrong. They say those same wheel-less natives literally could not see the square rigger ships in the bay and thought that the White people had magically appeared in the tiny row boats. They had no concept of sailing ships and they could not see them.

Now, think about going from there to trying to make them understand sailing. My thinking was torn between two worlds. Try as I might I would always be White. How do I unlearn concepts? I was looking for the shared experience to use as common ground. I will probably never understand the people I live amongst. (Anyway, what was the name of that Tom Hanks movie? Castaway?)

CHAPTER 64, DAY 222, STRESS

On day 222 I must have been in real trouble if I was still writing. Writing for three days in a row was a bad sign. My Spanish was terrible; the beer was served with ice, sunny and seventy six degrees, food in the fridge, roof over my head and more than enough clothes in the closet. What the heck more could a person need?

If I wrote for five days straight I wanted someone to call the guys in the white coats because it could only mean I had totally lost my grip on terra firma. I did stop myself from that obsessive need to find assurances from outside myself. I had all I needed; my life and person were complete and secure. I wanted for no more than I had. My eyes were filled with the vision of God's fine works around me in all their splendor and glory. I loved life.

I looked to see the molecules of life that existed between my eyes and that which they beheld. I was one with God and the universe supported me in every way. There only is. *Asi es* (So it is). My moment was happening now. I existed only to provide the service I had been brought forth to provide.

The choice was not mine. I was guided to fulfill a destiny that had been woven into the fabric of time long ago. I envied those of you who created your own reality. I guess it was your destiny to feel like you were making your life unfold. I felt like a skipping stone, only briefly touching down and even then touching down on a liquid surface.

I would warn the would-be expatriate that life was not going to be like you think it should when you lived in a strange land. Making my life take a direction was not as easy as it had previously been. I felt like what had happened was supposed to happen and maybe even more fatefully than earlier in my life.

I never would have chosen this path. I taught stress management classes in the US and I would not have wished this on anyone. In the last year: I quit my jobs, sold everything I own, sold my house, lost my dad, separated myself from all my friends, moved out of the country, began to learn a new language, lost my mom, bought a house, had my brother attempt to swindle me, made two international flights, started a new relationship, lost a new relationship, started a new home, started to learn how to use the internet, began international banking, changed my eating habits and God knows what I was forgetting.

I was blessed that I only once fell through the roof one time. By rights I should be stressed beyond any level of sound mental health. Thank God I knew just how bad off I had it. That gave me a generous amount of latitude in forgiving myself my sins. Believe me when I say I had sinned plenty. For the moment, I only had the moment. Nothing I was going to do could change the past.

People had been leaning on me hard and I could not fault them their perceptions. I could only do as Christ would do; I forgave myself. I was love. However messy, smelly, sticky and awkward as I could be; I would not be restrained. Not that I had anything to say about it because I believed it was my destiny. I was neither better than I could be nor any worse. I was as bad a person as I was and was only as good as I was fated to be.

I traveled down a road that was unknown and unclear. Try to bring as much of your culture with you as you can. I did not mean stuff. Bring the part that was greater, more personal and deeper than things. I guess it always gets back to bringing love with you. It was universal and accepted anywhere they accept Visa. Be sure to turn the fire hose of love on yourself regularly *y espera con esperanza* (and wait with hope).

CHAPTER 65, DAY 245, DAVID PANAMA

On day 245 I would have told you I didn't want to write anymore. I had made a commitment to the interested to continue. I lay across the balance of right effort and gave that devil its' due. I no longer lived to write. I had shifted somehow into the realization of another period of personal growth. The paradox of loss through gain always loomed overhead. You know... I may have grown nerves of steel but I mourned the loss of the old nerves. I lived in perpetual springtime yet I mourned the loss of winter snow.

Why was I feeling so nervy? Well, I had returned from a visit to Panama. That really did not say much. I did little but ride on busses and hangout in hotel rooms. For whatever reason I seemed to attract the company of young non American English speaking backpacker types. It was fun and enlivening to share time with these youths. The young men were full of self-confidence and surety, albeit without a fully developed understanding of the global nature of humanity. The young women were so sweet and so scared.

I probably could have just gone to the *frontera* (border) and caught the scene at the immigration office to form an opinion of Panama. What a mess. The 51 people on the bus were almost the only people there and it took two hours for the Panamanians to scan and stamp the passports. For whatever reason, they did not seem happy in their air-conditioned office with the world cup on the TV screen.

The *Ticos* were much friendlier than the Panamanians. I guessed that Panama had more of an urban interaction pattern and Costa Rica had a more rural and genteel communication style. The Panamanians were more indigenous looking than the *Ticos* and were not prone to excessive greetings. I could have even said they were more like the French than the Italians.

However, the *Gringos* in Panama were more loquacious and gracious than they were in Costa Rica. Maybe that was because I was traveling with lonely English speakers and the other people I met in a bar. I did not hang out in bars in Grecia. I'd have guessed the *Gringo* bar crowd in Grecia was more chatty and friendly than their coffee shop counterparts. I was missing out on a whole aspect of global culture by not being in the drinking scene. Or maybe the *Gringos* in Panama were more outgoing and the Panamanians were not.

David had a much more orderly and restrained atmosphere than Grecia. No kids were openly smoking dope in the park or whores hanging on the benches and strolling the walks. The city of David looked like it was clean, crisp and in good repair. It would have felt less contrived if it were in the US. The park in David would have seemed more relaxed and friendly if it were anywhere else in the world. However, it was a beautiful little park with ornamental palms, a water feature and colored lighting.

David was very Latin except for the good roads and sidewalks. They even had street signs and handicap curb cuts. In general, David was more American feeling. It was less crowded and more orderly and subsequently it felt safer. I probably felt safer on crowded streets than ones that were empty. David did not have the same bustle as in Grecia; the houses, like the people, were more spread apart.

As for the cost of living in Panama, it seemed as if rents and housing might be higher than Costa Rica. But, olive oil and salad dressing was much cheaper. Most groceries were 20% cheaper, but a few were the same or higher priced. There were more American brand names and a better selection in David than in Grecia. For the $120 I spent on travel and lodging, I turned it into a lucrative shopping trip. It felt like I would spend more money if I lived in Panama, due to the temptation to buy more, because it was cheaper. The price of goods in Costa Rica prevented me from buying many items.

CHAPTER 66, DAY 246, PIRATES OF THE CARIBBEAN

On day 246 I thought I might write about Costa Rica. [Isn't that why you were here? (Expat, Costa Rica, Cultural Adjustment, Retirement) Search!] It was interesting that *Gringos* were leaving Costa Rica to move to Panama. It was also interesting to see the types of people doing it and what they said.

Most of the folks moving to Panama that I met were rich kids. They were all grown now but still just playing like children with money. One gent in particular I found most interesting. He had spent seven years in Costa Rica and was married to a *Tica*. He built and sold an apartment building in San Jose and had monthly income from the sale. He looked to be 75 but was probably younger; the booze and the smokes were unkind to him. He was married to a 58-year-old *Tica* and they had no kids together.

He said "I will never step foot in Costa Rica again." He went on to add "They have no extradition there." He never told me exactly why that was important to him but he did mention that Costa Rican divorce laws favored women heavily. The spoken consensus was that it was 50/50 like in the States. The guys who had one, or who were trying to avoid one, said different. They said 80/20. Ouch…

Let me help to clarify the extradition comment. Extradition is an agreement between countries to exchange fugitives from justice. If a person who does something bad in Costa Rica might run to Panama, if they got caught they would be sent back if there was extradition. The reciprocal would also be true **if** an agreement was in place. Run rabbit run. If you mess up bad enough in Costa Rica you could always cross the border to start afresh.

He and the wife were off for a Colombian vacation then he was headed to *El Norte* to see his mom and dad. His folks were closing on ninety and he wanted to visit. The wife goes back to Costa Rica after the vacation and they stayed married. Ahhh...Life in the tropics: the unexpected and the unusual around every corner.

I did a little online research and learned how Costa Rica's Pacific coastline had once been a Pirate's Haven. Sir Francis Drake, Captain Morgan, Black Beard, Roberts and many others used Costa Rica as harbor to attack ships laden with silver from Mexico and gold from Peru. The Spanish were carting it across Panama and shipping it to Europe. The Caribbean side had their own set of pirates and stories of plunder. On both shores there were stories of golden treasures sunken off shore or buried on shore for later recovery. It seems that the treasure map had its' origin in fact.

The name Rich Coast did not help. The only gold work found in Central America was in Costa Rica during an exploration party from Panama. The word spread and treasure seekers came to Costa Rica to rob (I mean, trade with) the natives for their wealth. So, Costa Rica's founding European ancestors came to rob and plunder and it appeared from the looks of the offspring that they were predominantly Italian.

Well, far be it from me to make cultural slurs, generalizations or stereotypes. I would never... Though I must ask, "Have any of you seen the Godfather series?" The friendliness might outweigh the larceny and it was up to me to watch my treasures and protect their safety. I liked the outgoing nature of the people and I had to sort out the con artists from the genuine article.

As for history, what was past was past. In acculturating it was personally healthier for me to move forward than it was to cling to the familiar past. It just made me miss my previous life all the more. So eat local, buy local, be local and embrace the native life!

CHAPTER 67, DAY 250, GRECIA

On day 250, aside from having found a fourth marble, I was also turning another corner. Every 90-day cycle had a rhythm of its' own and some required more attention than a run for the border. I flew back to Oregon in September. Two glorious weeks in the chilly paradise awaited me.

There were return flights and ground transportation to arrange, pre-orders to be shipped to Oregon, hotels to book, plans to be made about spending time, documents prepared, flights confirmed and whatever else. The culture, the culture!

Aside from trip preparation I engaged in a new regimen that was conducive to organizing my time. I had begun work on a Grecia City mapping project in earnest. It put me on the street in the morning and left me with the afternoon to refresh, write or do whatever else that remained to be done. Preparatory activities and housekeeping were what I thought might take most of my time.

I was a one man spectacle in the mornings as I walked around the streets loitering long enough to write down the names of businesses. I guessed not many people walked around making notes in a note pad. They thought maybe I was the guy from National Geographic? In any event, I garnered more than my fair share of how-de-dos and only a few sideways glances.

I was pleased to note a large number of stores open at 8:00 AM and somewhat surprised to see lines forming at places which didn't open until 9:00 AM. I thought that project might have been my key to integration. From how quickly the project had gone I was uncertain if I would have enough exposure. I liked the morning air, the quiet in the streets and watching the downtown wake up to smoky trucks, boxes, and hand carts. The quiet lent itself to listing activity.

However, when researching the businesses, I had to be there at 10:00 or 11:00 AM. Researching the businesses would take an interpreter because some signs made no sense to me and I needed someone who could read Spanish better than I. The wandering into shops and asking if someone spoke English there… that would be the fun part. I looked forward to the moments of hesitation and them looking about the room for the one English speaker or the "just a little." *Todo bien*. What did you sell? Did you have a card with a phone number? *Tiene un buen dia. Gracias.* Oh what fun…? Hopefully this would be met with lots of smiling and laughing.

That part of the mapping project waited for my return from Oregon. The listing filled the morning hours and put me in the heart of town. It was like my morning walk in the hills of Cottage Grove Oregon. Waking up at 5:00 I still had three hours at home before the early stores opened. I had time for coffee, breakfast and washing a load of clothes. Mornings were often cool and overcast. The weather could break by 6:00 AM and it could be mighty warm by 8:00 AM. I liked the more deserted feeling in the streets.

There was a hidden incentive also. There were good pastry goods and *café con leche* (coffee with milk) to be had in Grecia Central. That ate into the pocket book and deposited it directly on my gut, however, it was incentive. I also found some specialty items. There were so many pastry shops, shoe stores and clothes shops and I did find a few points of interest. Many bakeries had one or two items the other shops did not have. I was on the lookout for a good baguette.

For a guy with a cloistered lifestyle and temperament, I sure did want to socialize. I was telling a virtual friend that morning (it was a real person on the phone) that upon my return from Oregon I would seriously consider abandoning all vestiges of virtual or long distance friendships and hoped the loss would force me into real relationships with real people on the streets

CHAPTER 68, DAY 254, METAPHORIC LIFE

Day 254 and we were all creatures of habit. Someone recently mentioned that we could create habits that we want to keep. I agreed and thought that we all did that. Good habits made for good outcomes…

I felt a commitment to myself to maintain the habit of writing every few days. I continued even though I was told that my writing would probably not be widely accepted. I guessed the rules of blogs were that they wanted puff pieces only and that nothing would be printed that could be construed to be derogatory. I didn't mean any harm to anyone but even I could look at my writing as derogatory… if I tried.

To wit: (when did I ever get to use that) I seemed to be finding myself living one of 4 metaphors. Three of them could be considered unflattering images of Costa Rican life. The forth metaphor was what I was here for. That day I thought of beachcombing and finding a great little surf town with a gentle winter swell and an uncrowned point break with long peeling six foot swells. Living here would have been so much more tolerable with surfing as a pastime. Once the residency papers were in place and I had my provisional residency card I would consider surfing in paradise.

On the new road to Jaco I was only an hour away from the swells. I found a surf and skate shop here in Grecia. Hmmm? I did not have to live at the beach. I could always go and visit when the swells were hitting. That was all a wonderful fantasy and that was the upbeat metaphor. However, the required trips over the border took some of the wonder and allure out of travel. As lush and beautiful as the scenery was it was nine to twelve hours of scenery in a cramped bus seat.

Sometimes I found myself walking down the street smiling. A bird would sing and my day instantly sparkled. Some odd moment would pass and I felt at ease and tranquil (from the word *tranquillo*). Save for the times I was frustrated and nothing seemed to reach completion' it could not be better. "It's the climate" as they boasted in Grants Pass Oregon. As pleasant and easy as the weather was I was transmuted into Steve McQueen in Papillion. I often thought of that movie, based on a true story, about a guy who kept escaping from the French Foreign Legion Prison. They stuck him on a tropical island with Dustin Hoffman. He still wanted to escape even though he lived in his own little paradise. He risked shark attack and drowning to leave his paradise island. Well, there was only one Great Escape and we each had to wait for our turn.

The third metaphor was of being locked up in a POW camp or prison. That feeling was partially caused by the bars on the windows and the high walls around the courtyard creating an un-climbable barrier from the street. Sometimes it felt like I was on shopping furlough and I was sneaking a smoke or a drink with the guys. I lived out the days on the calendar and counted them as they passed. I wondered how many days might remain. Well, I was only sentenced to 365 days of journaling. He he he.

Lastly, I had the feeling I had landed on Mars and it was not the planet but was the Martians who seemed weird to me. They were all so different, talked in unfamiliar ways, had odd ways of thinking and I felt lost in their land. They appeared friendly and nice and all, I just did not know my way around their world. Nothing was either familiar nor as it appeared to be from my earthly perspective.

These four different thought patterns occupied my mind regularly and I would not have said one was more dominate than another. I thought they were mostly situational and the triggers were difficult to discern. I found myself in a living in the moment culture with ever-changing conditions. I was without options really. I just made a go of it as best I could. The rumor was that 80% of expats who moved to Costa Rica washed out in the first two years. It sounded like just about everything else in life. I was here in Costa Rica and it was livable by American refugee standards and I had to love those rats in the gutters or I would have hated living here.

CHAPTER 69, DAY 257, WOMAN'S WORLD

On day 257 I started to notice that around July there was another cycle of spring. A wet spring but spring none the less. There were more butterflies. Trees filled with birds and squirrels looking for new berries, fruits and flowers. Those who said they missed the seasons did not look outside the windows of their temperature and humidity controlled homes.

There were four distinct seasons as the sun made its sweep up and down the latitudes. The beginning of a Northern summer was the wet season warming here. We had peak heat again in September as the sun passed heading south and the real rains came. In November the drying spring began again into the blistering heat of March.

I had little but I had ample time and creature comforts were attainable to those of even paltry means. I moved in on a $500 a month budget and did not use all of it. I lived poor by choice and not because the country was poor. Many people lived here with very American lifestyles. I was just cautious and watched to see what happened. The dollar bill was exchanging for fewer and fewer Colones and the unfavorable exchange rate was raising my monthly internet bill.

Costa Rica was a special place. For those northern red neck guys who debated with women in the US who thought women would do a better job running the world... Send those women to Costa Rica. It was a political and cultural system unlike even the surrounding countries. The people here were physically different from their neighboring counterparts. I imagined there had been a tremendous amount of inbreeding to get a country of people who looked markedly like each other, yet markedly different from the peoples in the neighboring countries. They kept things to themselves because security was important and they didn't intermingle.

This was a documented matriarchal society that had laws that favored women over men and there were even laws that said you had to be nice to people. They had a woman president and a culture that supported flights of fancy. They still used the family name following the mother and property was handed down accordingly. Straight answers? They were few and far between. In the north we used "he" to refer to neutral gender and here they used "she."

There were holes in the roads and every business transaction was painfully drawn out and tediously slow albeit very sociable. No one was willing to take responsibility for their actions and many people must be involved in every part of every business interaction. In Costa Rica there was no military, but there was a huge social welfare debt that was supported only by taxing the working class. As a country they had no business sense for succeeding in the global market place.

Like all things related to women I had to sigh and ask "Wasn't that just beautiful?" There was something beautiful about a long line of teenagers with babies in their arms waiting at an *economico social* office. Costa Rica does have a system to support the social welfare of unwed mothers. I had to wonder if those girls become mothers just to bring an extra income into the household.

Oh the beautiful female intention…One day those gals were going to send their guys to fix the roads in Costa Rica. How was it that their poorer neighboring countries could manage to maintain their roads in much better condition than Costa Rica could?

CHAPTER 70, DAY 259, STUDYING SPANISH

The weather interested me more than studying did. I had heard thunder before in different places in the US and abroad. It had never been like the thunder I heard in Costa Rica. I enjoyed the rain. But the thundering… that was a good time of day to shower and change, study Spanish, cook, clean or write.

Eventually I typed my street findings and that was not as fun as the hour or two on the streets every morning. Yard work filled the void and I did not find myself with an excess of time. (Except on that day everything happened quickly. Map work 45 min, coffee and cornbread 20 min and Maxi shopping in ten minutes with no waiting in line.) That day I actually did dishes in hot water the old camp stove way by heating a pot of water. I had some oily pans and it was the only time I had not washed dishes in cold water. I did use a heated shower, but many *Ticos* just used cold water showers.

I was writing to avoid studying Spanish. I understood what I understood. I blended as best I could and I didn't look backward. Those living a Northern lifestyle in Costa Rica, if they could speak Spanish or not, were doing so on more than $400 a month.

I had learned a few niceties and had passable *tienda* Spanish; so, if the store clerk was motivated to sell me something they would understand my Spanish. There were some locals who tolerated my baby talk. Every now and then I was able to practice my ignorance. It became obvious that fitting in was really not realistic without excellent Spanish and great social skills.

I could still be here and not fit in. I kept learning more Spanish and that smoothed out a few of the bumps in the road. I was closer to having a *Tico* (rather than a *Gringo*) income but I still would not fit in. That was OK. My budget was another one of the great compromises that made living in paradise possible for me.

Writing was a diversion from my newly intended and self-imposed conviction to improve my Spanish. My plan was to put time into the program that brought my Spanish to where it was: Rosetta Stone. On the bus to Panama I had been catching up on the audio refreshers that I loaded into the MP3 player. I lost an MP3 but I had a copy on the laptop so I listened to the refreshers then started back to new lessons. The lessons were becoming very challenging so it was easy to find other excuses not to devote time to intentional study. Immersion was good, however study was better...

I had my morning map project that ran me into people and I would occasionally hang out with them and chat. The transient *Gringo* population accepted me more readily than the old timers. I just went with what I received. I didn't understand the social life of a *Tico* and *Gringos* had their own clicks already. Most *Gringos* did not appear of interest to me or interested in meeting me. After all, I did not ask their permission to live in their town.

CHAPTER 71, DAY 265, FRIENDS

I was writing on day 265 merely because I had not written for almost a week. (What would have happened if I had never written again?) The little worried soul that bought a round trip ticket to the human experience was still white knuckling it out on the merry-go-round of life. Whatever it was I had been worrying about for all these many years was finally at a point far enough away I could begin to focus my farsighted vision on it. The problem was that it was so far away I could not discern the details. Oddly enough I often worried about what I could not control and I did not worry about that which I could take action.

I heard they determined that pre-natal nail biting occurs in babies. I was not going to write about my old family life. However, my new Costa Rican new family was as crazy as the old family. I had written about Jim (though he might not have been of sound judgment, he was of affable disposition and met many people). Jim said I was right about the *Gringos* here being a bit unusual, a little fruity, left of center and one sandwich short of a picnic kind of crazy.

I sometimes heard Johnny Depp's voice as he played Hunter S. Thompson in Fear and Loathing in Las Vegas and fancied myself with a cigarette holder and martini pecking away poorly at the keys. (The guy was a two finger typist for Pete's sake.) Flights of fancy were all that seemed to be left to me as I took my joy from a future yet to unfold.

Was this where *Gringos* went to find center or did they go to Costa Rica to just quietly slip over the edge? I heard many stories of Fear and Loathing in Costa Rica in the form of alcohol abuse, drugs, girls, scams, larceny and theft. Sexual perversions and drinking seemed high on the list of *Gringo* interests and pastimes. So, that left the *Ticos* for friends.

The whole town of Grecia seemed to take on a mood sometimes and the people responded accordingly. I was too old school for the US and I am way too conservative for this wild-west part of the world. Life went on.

I was developing a friendship with a gal who had a shop on my walking path to my house. That shop gal, who spoken English with me, closed her shop and moved out of town. Now my daily walk to town was not met with a chance greeting or a moment to rest and chat.

In January I wrote about a gal who was trying to help me by translating at a fruit stand. Though I looked at her many times I could not tell anything about her. When my shopping was done she was gone from sight and mind.

Now, it seemed I might be developing another *Tica* friendship. This new shop gal was just a face. When I first saw her that was all I noticed. I had seen her mopping or sweeping in the front of the shop and I could not tell you if she was skinny or fat, top heavy or slight of build as I had no clue. She spoke no English but she was making an effort to understand my Spanish and that was worth the world.

I worked on the Grecia directory as if it would matter. I cannot imagine it being very useful in a year or two when the stores change again. Everything was for sale or rent. I saw many vacant store fronts and houses for sale for too long a period of time. Panama had lower unemployment and less reported crime than Costa Rica. I thought that maybe the US economic decline had really hurt Costa Rica and it was showing.

CHAPTER 72, DAY 268, MY BIRTHDAY

It was day 268 and I was way behind in my writing. The word count was down and I was preoccupied and otherwise distracted. Odd, I had a goal of reducing virtual communications and to go native and I had a writing goal which had me scripting virtual communications. I logged my birthday in e-mails to Christine and I pasted them below:

PETER: I just cried I was so touched. Thanks for making the effort to send that card. I know you put some thought into picking that card. *Usted es muy amable.* (You are very kind.) I was going out for a *Tico* breakfast. I worked on the map and felt sorry for myself…oh well, I couldn't change everything. Yours were nice thoughts and we would see what unfolded for today. Probably not much, considering my mood.

PETER: Did I forget to mention that I would intersperse moments of bliss and eternal gratitude in with the self pity…it all comes and goes. I was going to buy an office chair or two to make my life more comfortable. I was thankful for you at this moment in time…Peace Out

PETER: I had more time than I thought. I took too much time here and had to wait until 1:00 for the stores to open and the *soda* (café) to slow down. Was I going to let them cook lunch too? I was not hungry right then, but I wanted Tiramisu. I had the Italian make a pizza for me; then, I looked for Tiramisu. Yea I was going to buy a chair for my birthday; it just looked like I was not buying today. I might go look at another set I liked that cost $150. It was a little out of town and a bus or five dollar taxi each way. Looooooong walk. I walked the big loop of it last year and I had blisters on my toes and heels. It was not the most grueling loop I ever walked but it was the second most grueling.

PETER: The chairs I saw ranged from $30 to $200? That can't be right. The numbers were real weird in Costa Rica, i.e. 2.005 was two thousand and five thousand. It could have been right. It was nice just not that nice. The comparable high end office chairs were selling for $60 to $80. I offered $100. Let's see that was roughly cinquenta mil, fifty mil or 50.000 Colones. They were asking 56.400 with the 20% discount for cash. Manana... Well the Italian was not busy and I heard the rumble of thunder already at 12:28 and it was graying...Gotta run

PETER: The chair store did not open until 1:30 and I was there at 1:00. The Italian made me the bacon onion mushroom pizza with red sauce. His red sauce was so rich it burned my mouth. That day I was home in the rain. Mushrooms and onions were good. I really liked the quick east coast mind of that New Jersey expat. He lived on the fringe of the *Gringo* world and today revealed to me that he had a mentor six years ago who advised him to avoid the *Gringo* crowd. The mentor was a financially successful 30-year expat living in Costa Rica. *Bueno*....three people thought the *Gringo* scene was very inbreed *if ya nos wat i means*. I hoped I never became one of the Italian's stories. He was full of good observations. It seemed he was basing them on decades of someone else's research. When I met people who were adjusted to *Tico* living I listened to them. It seemed like he did the same.

PETER: Your wish came true and a Blackhawk stalled overhead and sung a sharply whistled song. At the same time a Kite (another hawk all in white) was doing its own stalling dance off in the distance. That was always one of my favorite sightings. Later a blue Morpheus, the butterfly of the movie "Papillion," flew past my window and then back again. A young girl working in the grocery (Discount Thursday) wanted help learning her Spanish pitch in English. It was a fun day after all!

They had tiramisu at the *Panaderia*. I was going to buy one and had the gal cut it and I shared the slice with her because she had been so nice. I went to pay for my *torta de cumpleano.* (birthday cake) and she said it was *gratis*. I opened the box of merlot I purchased for your cancelled visit and that made me teary eyed as I toasted the rain of the late afternoon and ate and drank and the tiramisu was waiting in the freezer. There was Spanish to study, no movies to watch and no grass to pull out of the garden. Thanks for being part of my birthday Christine...

CHAPTER 73, DAY 274, SELFLESS GIVING

On day 274 if I had something to learn here in Costa Rica, and I was sure I had more than one lesson to learn, it had something to do with selfless giving. I had volunteered to help Carlos with an electrical installation at his rental place and there was a story. I was going to the bus stop with no expectation of my friend arriving, and if he did it would be a big plus.

I had given him a shopping list and he told me that the shower was the last project to complete and that he had the parts. So, we did meet at the bus stop and he said we had to stop at the hardware store first. I could tell this three hour job was probably going to take a bit longer. Of course I would have liked to have made a list of the hardware I needed if we were going to go out of our way to go to "Home Depot" (here it was called EPA). Of course I received no advance warning of the changes. He did not think about the helper, it was just about him. He now wanted me to go to the hardware store and too bad if there was something I might want there. Oh Well, I remembered I needed a desk lamp and bought one! What else did I need for my house? No one else cared but me.

Now at Carlos' rental he was nowhere near move-in ready. The one hour shower install was followed with three hours of general cleaning and then it was raining. I had to carry my tools as we walked the streets looking for bus stops in which we would stand in the rain. It was after 3PM and I expected rain by that time of day. I just expected to be home by then. Carlos was leaving his tools in the house and he had his cousin drive a car there to pick up his things so they would not get wet. This type of thoughtless behavior was contagious and *Gringos* were equally self indulgent and the native culture said "So what?"

The *Gringo* John had a *Tica* chick for sex. Flor was a run-around girl who changed guys every few months or weeks. In the States she would be called a tramp but when a 60-year-old guy was having sex with a 30-year-old gal he called her a girlfriend. She grew tired of him soon enough and dumped him for the married taxi driver who was her lover when she and John first met But John "loved her" or so he said. He had a funny way of expressing love for the girl he would "kill for." Notice, I did not say he would die for her but he said he would have been happy to be hurtful in her name.

Wait, it got better, here was the good part. One day after he had been with some other gal for three months John called Flor on her cell-phone and offered to buy her lunch and pay for a taxi. That way she could put her kids on the bus and beat the bus home in the taxi after lunch. When she finished talking to John she put her kids on a bus and went to the bar where John had offered to buy her lunch and she ordered a ceviche and a beer (John also told me this same story himself). No sooner had she ordered lunch he asked her how she was going to pay for it. Lunch came, she ate, they talked, she asks for the lunch and taxi money and John screams at her "NEVER, NEVER, NEVER." Well, that gal was an unemployed mother of two, ages 8 and 11, as well as supporting her mother who was living at home.

Even if she was a tramp she deserved to be treated better than that. Why would someone who had perpetual income offer to help another person and then just stiff them? That seemed odd. She had to work for five hours to make enough money to cover the cost of lunch and a cab. At $1.80 an hour it takes a long time to earn an inexpensive lunch. John once said his time was worth $250/hour. So, if he were to compensate her equally, he owed her $1,250.00. He he he.

Both parties gave me the same story. She was angry and he was gloating about his inflicting emotional and financial pain on her. He said he would make it right for her...I could only laugh out loud at that thought. That was another example of the worst aspects of the culture being adopted by the *Gringos* who came here. *Ticos* could be cruel and self-centered by *Gringo* standards and the drunks and ner-do-wells who moved here felt like they were finally home. That guy stiffed me, too but for $150. Personally I felt like I was lucky that he stole from me as I then had good reason not to associate with him.

CHAPTER 74, DAY 275, *TICO* DIRECTIONS

On day 275 I was again headed to the bus stop to meet friends. We had made plans to go to *un parque en las montanas* (a park in the mountains). They both actually showed for the 9:30 bus which was a small miracle for Jim who drinks all day and usually sleeps 12 to 14 hours a night. Even though Carlos does not appear to be a drunk and had grown up in Grecia and Carlos first took us to the wrong bus.

The bus driver told Carlos it was the next bus. Carlos said we had to wait for an upcoming bus. But I noticed the name of the city we wanted on the "next bus over." We got onboard that bus easy enough and an hour later we were in Poas where we change busses to Fraijanes. Carlos again asks the *chauffer* (driver) for directions to catch the connecting bus and Carlos told us that the driver said "Right here." We pile out and Jim lights a smoke and they want to mill around and wait "right there" for the next bus when I could see a sign 20 meters ahead for the town we wanted.

Finally we were headed up the mountain, or I should say volcano, and the clouds were thicker and the sky was grayer. With Carlos as our trusty guide we were going somewhere. Jim asked Carlos how he knew about that park and he said he rode his bicycle some grueling double century down from San Ramon to San Jose over Poas and home. We *Gringos* were all high fives, attaboys and "I thought I was tough."

In Fraijanes, Carlos was again confused and asked directions from a local. (Remember when I said ask three locals directions and receive three sets of directions.) According to a store owner, we had past the park by three kilometers. I was unsure which park because I did not see any signs for a park in the last five miles but it was all downhill, even if it was raining…

A couple of miles into walking down hill and Jim prompted Carlos to ask another person on the street for directions to the park. She said "Go back uphill to town and just next to the trout pond with the restaurant resort was a forest park." I even vaguely remember reading about that one in the Lonely Planet book. When we walked past the trout pond going downhill, I pointed it out as a place to visit, fish, have trout cooked and they said something about trails in the book. OK it sounded right to me.

We headed back up the hill and the rain lightened a bit. Now, I was a tad warm in a raincoat but Carlos had no umbrella and was using mine. Upon reaching the trout pond, as Jim stood in the rain, I sought shelter in a bus stop (many rural bus stops had covers and some even had walls). While checking the time and discussing our options Carlos took it upon himself to ask a third person for directions. She said that we had to catch a bus on a side-route to Alajuela from there and the El Lago Park was on that route.

We had left at 9:30 and it was now 1:00 PM and the last bus downhill, in daylight, was at 3:30. Were we going to start another mystery adventure? Carlos was game for a bus tour. He could catch up on his much needed sleep. Jim would suffer nicotine cravings and I boredom as we explored the unknown? No, let's save it for another time and head back down the hill toward home.

Further down the hill it was sunny and warmer. We had passed another park I would have liked to have seen that was on a more frequent bus route, every half-hour rather than every two hours. Carlos said it was close to the *Parada* (bus stop) and yes it was only a 1000 yards from the stop. We made the walk to the free (only charged on Sunday) park that would be a great event grounds. We rambled and meandered, but no one wanted to walk up river on what appeared to be a well established trail.

Lollygagging around watching Jim chain smoke and down beers was not my reason to go to a park. However, it was beautiful and there was a bar, restaurant, swimming pool, basketball court and an old sugarcane mill museum in Spanish. So, we remained there for a couple of hours until it was dumping rain and no one was prepared for rain but me. They want to take a ten dollar taxi home because they were not prepared for rain in the rainy season. Leave it to a drunk and a *Tico* to turn a simple two dollar trip to a trail to a seven dollar mystery adventure. "I'm on the road to nowhere."

P.S. Carlos later said that he had only gone there by bus from Alajuela and was unfamiliar with today's approach. What bike ride? I just had to laugh and smile because it was so entertaining.

CHAPTER 75, DAY 278, SOMETIMES DEPRESSING

I usually started my day at 6:00 AM after my first coffee and having watched the sunrise through the back window. The sky had already been bright for an hour and it was a coastal 70 degrees. That day had been christened financial review day. The day I looked at all my account activity online (internet permitting), updated registers, made phone calls, made corrections, and then breathed a sigh of relief.

I had plans. I had plans to write a guide to Grecia for tourists Maybe I could sell it to rich *Gringos* who live in the hills and surrounding communities. But mostly I wrote it for me. When I visited in March of 2009 I noticed there were no street names or numbers and that the stores and services were difficult to locate. I wrote about locals making up their own language, they also made up their own directions. Good directions were rare. Service directories did not exist and stores carried the most unusual mixes of merchandise. I wanted to make a map for myself of where the stores were so I could find them again later. I thought it would be worth some money to folks who came to town to shop. It would have given me an excuse to approach *Gringos* on the street. It had given me an exercise program. Best of all, I could later find the shops where English was spoken and it was a chance to meet most of the local vendors.

The rain was taking a toll on my outdoor activity. I felt like I needed to stop eating so my calorie intake more closely matched my calorie output. As for meeting people here in Costa Rica... the whole relocation process had been so guided I could not take credit for making anything happen in regards to my being here. This was also true in terms of meeting people. I had been flying on faith and I believed I met the people I was supposed to meet. It seemed like there were a myriad of lessons to be learned.

I had discovered another reason I was not clicking with the *Gringos*. I believed they were here because they wanted to live in a land of drunks and pirates. It fit their personalities. I did not want to live here but was forced here by fiscal necessity. No one seemed to understand that. The grass was only greener because Costa Rica was full of manure and it rained much of the time. Ha ha ha ha.

It was with suspended judgment that I kept my judgment up front and out in the open. That was a long story... I had and held my judgments and used them to guide my actions because judgment gave me the ability to anticipate reactions. We all already knew everything there was to know. It was just a matter of accepting the truth, not as I wanted it to be but as it was. Allowing myself to be right about being judgmental was quite liberating.

Back to the weather... I had the blues because I was human. The gray sky only seemed to begin the cycle. The miracle seemed to lie in being happy with the fact that I had desires. I might or might not acquire what I wanted but I was accepting the outcome if it favored me or not. Loving me was great and admirable; I thought it came right after accepting me. (Was that not correct? Did accepting myself remove any possibility of self-criticism?) I was making the effort to just say *Asi es*, not only in terms of others but also in terms of me. I surmised that being in Costa Rica made me even more tolerant. Accepting certain people for friends could start to make me look good to myself. If they were OK then I must be a saint on earth.

I had my days of distress but I mostly accepted they were an inevitable part of the process. I had a Zen retreat idea: no tools, no machines, no cooking, no work, and the no human contact. That meant no Internet, walks, shopping distractions, talking, electrical communications or devices. It would be a day with nothing to do and no one to focus on. The Jews focused on God and the Buddhists focused on no thought and I... I would figure that out. LOL

CHAPTER 76, DAY 285, *TICO* BUSINESS

On day 285 my life was very quiet. Some might have called it boring. Jim called my life boring but I thought he was rather boring himself. That day the guy complained how he only saw two hours of sun a day. If I woke up at nine and ventured outside at ten I would only see two hours of bright sun. The *Ticos* and I rose at five and watched the sun come over the ridge at six. I saw six hours of sun a day. If the afternoon had some more clearing, and it often did, then I saw even more sunshine.

I was no longer going out at dawn to work on the maps; that part had been finished. I went out after nine; when the stores were open, to confirm my notes. All the data was logged into the laptop and working copies of the maps had been printed, I had reviewed 13 of the 17 maps and updated and corrected my working drafts.

Interestingly enough I found a staggering two percent of the businesses that I had previously located 3 weeks earlier were closed. Two percent per month was 24% a year. I imagined that the truth of the matter was that nearly half of the businesses changed hands before a year was complete. It was not a matter of poor economy as in the north; I believed it was the result of poor business planning.

I supposed that businesses were opened under delusions of grandeur. Perhaps the entrepreneurs ignored the facts and just went forward based on their ego-centered desires. Desire for profit alone was insufficient strategy to run a business and the doors closed. Soon enough another wide-eyed delusional started a new shop in that location with dreams of riches and income without effort.

Soon after opening they folded too, owing rent and inventory costs and so what. No one seemed to care about tomorrow or credit references or money in the bank. Somehow, a small thought was turned it into a fact and then they were disappointed when their version of the truth was not transformed into reality. Jose who had worked for me was somewhat typical. He said he was going to open a bar with no money because he could borrow the tables and chairs and the beer company was going to give him the beer on credit. This reality only existed in his head since there was no free beer.

I told him that I was going to the US and might need a house-sitter. With that information alone, he had that he was the person who I was going to have housesit for me... even after he had stolen money from me. He thought I would still want him to have free reign of my house and my belongings. He kept asking about it and I finally told him it was not a possibility and he stopped coming to work for me.

A gal I was paying by the hour to help me look for houses was angry when I bought from an agent she had not met. Apparently one agent offered her a finder's fee and when I found a house with another agent she was upset. She had wanted the additional $500 on top of the money I had paid her by the hour. Then we were no longer friends and whatever other business I had for her was lost. There was a feeling of entitlement in Costa Rica that went beyond any reasonable or rational thought. Even some panhandlers became angry if they did not receive money on demand.

When I had an offer in on the Casa Rosa but I kept looking at other houses. One guy kept asking me when I was going to buy his house. It did not matter how many times I told him I had an offer pending he kept pushing as if we had an agreement to buy his house. (Was that delusional or what?)

The Realtors on Casa Rosa had overcharging the seller $5,000 in commissions. My Realtor then had the nerve to ask me for an extra $2,500 and when I said, "No," she became huffy. I offered to talk to the selling agent for her and she quickly said "No" and did not want to discuss the facts. It was that same thinking that had all these stores opening and then closing and who knew how bad the behind the scenes. business was.

CHAPTER 77, DAY 288, TOURIST VERSUS RESIDENT

It was day 288 and time flew and I was flying too. In September I made a flight to the northlands and had yet another chance to visit the land of high speed, bright lights and great expanses... It would not be as daunting the second time. However, I was still not a good traveler.

I had a residency application file number now and there was a rumor that I was able to stay in-country without visa renewal trips. I wondered why I was going to spend all that time and energy traveling to the farthest away spot in the States. (Did I miss my friends and American life so much I just couldn't stay away any longer?)

Well, there were a number of reasons for a return flight. I still had business in the States. I still had luggage in the States. And I still wanted to shop for more *Gringo* goods. My friends could come visit me... (They all thought this was paradise so why weren't they here?) There were also some practical advantages to keeping my tourist status here in Costa Rica.

I know I am repeating myself but it was necessary to leave the country every three months to maintain 90 day tourist visa status and legal visitation rights. Tourists had certain privileges that residents did not have. As a tourist I was allowed to bring personal property or have it shipped to Costa Rica for personal use tax free. Considering the tariff was usually equal to the purchase price of the item it represented a substantial savings. More importantly I was eligible for free medical care as a tourist.

The free medical care goes beyond the local clinic treatments that I had received in the past. The Hospital Mexico in San Jose had a mandate to treat tourists at no cost. It was said that the hospital was built with money from Mexico with the tourist treatment mandate. That was even better than the $40 a month national insurance because that was a major hospital with first class service. OK, maybe it was only second class service but it was not the third class service I received at the clinic.

You needed your original passport with a current visa stamp for services in the hospital. You also needed your original passport for business in the Bank. Your color copy will be accepted for most business transactions and in-country travel but the bank wants to see the real thing. I you did not take my advice and needed to cash traveler's checks or change Dollars into Colones you needed to stand in line with your passport in the bank. Of course you would also need the real thing to cross the border or for driving rental cars. With your US driver's license and original passport you are legal to drive in Costa Rica.

One day I had forgotten my passport for my banking adventure and I had to walk home for my papers before I did my bank business. I had accounts in the bank and ATM cards but the bank was very fussy and even needed to make a copy my passport in the process of our business. If you lost your passport or it expired there was help at the American Embassy of whatever country you are in. I take special care to protect my passport and only carry it when need be and good luck if you need Embassy help. I have neither heard nor read of anyone enjoying their Embassy experiences.

I wanted to share an interesting phenomenon I had observed at the bank. I was smart and I did not bring travelers checks and I avoided having to wait in the ridiculously long lines at the bank. I had my ATM card and I still had to take my place in the queue to use one of the machines. I banked at a branch of the Banco National that had inside ATMs. Most other banks had small glass rooms that house individual machines.

There were five machines in the foyer of the bank and taped out lines to help form a waiting line. It was incomprehensible why people would often be backed up in the queue waiting when four of the five ATMs would stand unused. (You tell me why! Was it a lucky machine? Were there bad experiences at the other machines? Could it have been engrained behavior patterns? Were there specific service machines? I just didn't get it. The other machines worked fine…why did they only want that one machine?)

Sometimes, people would wave me forward to the other machines but for the most part they would just ignore the rest of the line and wait. This was akin to the walking down a busy sidewalk and suddenly stopping for no apparent reason to stare off in the distance or standing in groups blocking the sidewalk. My advice, just push forward and take an empty ATM. No one would say anything.

I remember being on a long bus ride and I had a seat but I was trying to get an older gal's attention to offer her my seat. I was traveling with my friend Jose and he said "Don't." Courtesy was a hard habit to break but I could have left my courtesy in the States and my expectations of courtesy along with it.

CHAPTER 78, DAY 290, DIRT

It was day 290 and here was the dirt. (You thought I had been giving the low down and dirty story about Costa Rica? Well, I hadn't even started.) I was talking about plain old dirt. Well, maybe it was not plain or old but it was dirt none the less.

`I painted the Casa Rosa roof white a few months ago and it was now covered with soot. Yea, black gritty gunk that turned a white roof into a grey one at best. I cleaned the ceiling fan three or four weeks ago and did the same yesterday and pulled dust lions off of the blades. There were great globs of greasy glop on the leading edges and trailing over the blades.

I thought a place where it rained almost every day would have had clean fresh air but no. The windows were impossible to keep clean and I had to wonder about the source of all that flying debris. There was no industry in Grecia and not much in all of Costa Rica. We were not in the middle of farmland and the roads were paved.

There was the occasional burning of the sugarcane fields in the dry months but that had stopped back in May. OK, the trucks and busses puke out black exhaust even after their annual government inspection. (Amazingly the exhaust looked clean to an inspector.) Was that enough to create such "dirt?"

This was another phenomenon that escaped my logic. I guessed we were in the jet stream of some other third world industrialized nation that was burning coal and making steel. Were those pesky Africans making a mess of Central and South American coastal towns? I only ask that because of the trade wind patterns that cross the Atlantic.

I had a story of interest completely unrelated to the dirt. I met someone! A Costa Rican gal., they call them *Ticas* here. She was petite and cute and we met on one of my morning map making walks. I thought it was going somewhere because it seemed like we had a good connection without even exchanging words.

I had just started my six block map review and was probably going to be circling streets for an hour or two. She was just as sweet as could be and walked along with me as I check my type written draft for errors and changes. When I stopped she stopped with me. When I crossed the street she came along too. We really seemed to be compatible but I began to feel concerned she might want to go home with me because I was in no hurry to become too close too fast.

Well, it was fun while it lasted. Yes, past tense. It only lasted until I arrived at a hardware store in which I wanted to check on some prices for the Italian who was looking for a fixture for the restaurant. We stopped at the door and I asked her to wait because they probably would not like dogs in the store. When I left the store my new friend was nowhere to be found.

I was just feeling like I had sentenced myself to a life of solitary confinement when that dog decided to be my best friend and companion for an hour. But in typical *Tica* fashion if I was out of sight I was out of mind. It was sweet while it lasted and I just had to take what came my way, when it came my way. People did not look back or forward too much here. Apparently that went for the dogs too.

Seriously, I did not know if I had the cultural awareness or ability for a life here that was not one of solitude and melancholy. I did my best to have *Tico* friends. I was just not well adjusted enough to the differences and I felt awkward and disconnected. Well, I was not that well adjusted before I came here. So why should things be any different in Costa Rica than they were in the US.

CHAPTER 79, DAY 292, KINDNESS

On Day 292 I wondered about kindness as it worked in Costa Rican culture. I had spoken with the Italian... he and his female companion had been here six years and had a restaurant in order to keep themselves busy (they said they didn't need the money). I told him I had just realized that I would probably never have any friends here and that was a big pill to swallow. OK, he had good Spanish and frequent contact with *Gringos* and *Ticos* alike. Well, he became all teary eyed and said "Yea, you are exactly correct about that."

For a guy who always found it effortful to make friends it looked like I picked the wrong part of the world to improve those skills. Next life I was going to live in Canada. I really loved the people I met when I was there. After traveling in British Colombia I had often said "If not for the weather I would live in Canada. I loved the people." Canadians seemed to me to be genuinely open, honest, trusting and generous of spirit. If Americans were a few steps above the Latin people in that respect then the Canadians were at the top of the escalator. (But, what was that expression about having what I wanted or wanting what I have?)

I guessed I was supposed to develop a hardness that I was not able to create in *El Norte*. Openness came easy to me. Being closed was a talent that would have served me well in the US and would have saved me a bunch of grief in my life there. In Costa Rica hardness was a necessary survival technique.

I thought my personality had always been too soft. Nice guy complex. I was always told if I would be nice to others then they would be nice to me. That never worked up North so surely it would not work here. (OK Dr. Phil, don't ask, "How's that working for you?") I was not going to burden you with examples but it had just never worked all that well.

Here expressions of kindness were perceived as signs of weakness or opportunities to ask for more. It was almost like (if I performed some kindness) I must have been some kind of idiot or I had some hidden agenda. When I was living at the hotel one of the Nicaraguan guys that worked there offered me a coffee one morning. Later that day I gave him a couple of oranges for him and his coworker. The next morning he was knocking on my door asking for oranges. What's that? I gave what I felt I could spare and I was not trying to set a pattern of perpetual gifts.

I had been told not to give money to the bums in the park who panhandle because if I gave money to one they would all start hounding me for money every time they saw me. I would become the lucky ATM machine. Many *Gringos* were here because they fit into a pirate mentality or at least self-centeredness. It often seemed it was all take, take and take.

Jim wanted to teach a stained glass class, and I had a book with some 50 glass terms in Spanish and English. One morning I was looking for an excuse to go for a walk and I figured I could help him. So one Sunday I spent 45 minutes walking around with my book looking for an open copy center to make him a copy of the page of terms. Well, he looked at it and tossing it aside, promptly announced "This was not what I wanted." It seemed he wanted an entire lesson plan scripted out in Spanish and English. Well, sooooooorrrryyy, guess my efforts to be helpful were not good enough and therefore deserving of scorn.

For those of you needing to hear something nice, the weather was lovely and the people were full of kind greetings, big smiles and stated generosity. My interactions with women here were both beautiful and entirely depressing at the same time.

CHAPTER 80, DAY 294, PERSONAL GROWTH

On day 294 I had Zen on my mind. Now, for those who know of Zen, that alone was a paradox. Perhaps that was another aspect of the Expat experience. I could not leave this page blank and still convey the message. So I used these inadequate words to express those indescribable thoughts. (It sounded like a bunch of do do, didn't it?) Well, it was a bunch of dung and another part of the paradox. It was only with good fertilizer that one could grow good crops. However, I had to muck my way through the dung to find the riches and abundance that was there.

Some days it all seemed too much and then I realized the beauty of the absurd. I had made a friend of a *Tica* who, for whatever reason, would call me in the morning. I enjoyed talking to her because it was good Spanish practice and I enjoyed the sweetness of her voice. The conversation was mostly about her past *Gringo* husband and what a disappointment he was and how she did not trust *Gringos*.

This was *muy* Zen because I was not even trying to understand. Not trying and not understanding…very Zen. Acceptance was the lesson. Accepting what? Well, I accepted the paradox of her calling someone she did not "like." I accepted she was in pain. I accepted that I was a safe paramour because her heart was set against *Gringos*. More importantly I accepted that I didn't need to be the target of her angst and bitterness. There were plenty of other *Gringos* she could lambast.

I had mentioned the paradox of great displays of friendliness and camaraderie that were not followed by any welcoming behaviors. I also mentioned the illumination of illusion. Most of what was here was not as it appeared. Friends turned out to be thieves in the waiting. Good deals turned out to be rip-offs. Agreements turned out to be lip service. There was so much to accept in such a short time.

I received an opportunity to practice living without expectations every day and practice I did. Sometimes I saw the absurdity of my thinking and my northern culture logic. I caught myself asking a *Tica* to tell me if there was something I was doing that she did not like. Well, it was very *Tico* to say yes to everything so she said "Yes" that she would tell me if I were doing something she did not like.

Of course she told me what I wanted to hear "Yes," she said she would say "No" to me. I could see the absurdity of my question? What could I do about it? Well, I was watching what I asked. It was tough, but I somehow needed to ask questions that cannot be answered yes or no. The reason that was tough was because my Spanish was far from fluent and I often phrased my questions so I did not have to translate the answers.

Instead of asking "What do you want to do?" which might create a string of unfamiliar words, I would ask, "Do you want to go to lunch?" Those types of questions set me up for the "yes" answer, and the "no" behavior. I had grown a little smarter. When asking Flor to come clean the house I did not offer her a day and time to come to work rather I asked her when she wanted to work. If I asked her to come at a certain day or time she said "yes" and acted "no."

People said that dealing with Costa Ricans was like dealing with children and indeed, it was. Weirdly, neither their amount of education nor professional status changed that behavior. The factor that seemed to affected Costa Rican behavior most was whether or not they had lived in the US for any length of time.

People who had raised children had an easier time here if they kept that in mind. Expats who had not raised children were at a distinct disadvantage in Costa Rica. There was a certain beauty and innocence in the Costa Rican behavior albeit nerve racking at times.

CHAPTER 81, DAY 296, ONLINE SHOPPING

Day 296 and "What we have here is a failure to communicate." That was a movie line that seemed to apply to my experience being a first time online airgun buyer. There was more information out there than I could shake my checkbook at but clear and concise information was difficult to find. Sorting out fact from fiction was my primary focus as a first time airgun buyer.

I was an average Joe looking to continue my target shooting. Here in Costa Rica shooting opportunities were lacking so I began looking into airgunning as an alternative to firearms. Almost any online search for pellet guns, airguns, bb guns, airgun tuning, airgun parts or airgun dealers produced more blogs, forums and alleged directories than "results."

You might avoid the blogs and forums until you were done researching. If you were the least bit squeamish about killing birds and small animals or about breaking city ordinances or fish and game regulations you might form a poor opinion of air gunners from reading blogs and forums. Your time can be spent better than to spend it reading blogs and forums.

The people who helped me in my search for target shooting air guns seemed to be of a caliber similar to the firearm folks I met while in the gun business: kind, gentle, giving and responsible. I had nothing but praise for the responsible professionals who were providing services to airgun customers. After the guns left the store or shop... well, it took all kinds of people to make up the world.

The online directories were full of shops that were out of business or without addresses. There were also shops out of the country that popped up, and I couldn't tell until I saw the prices were in Pounds Sterling or Dollars Canadian.

I went to dealer websites to find the best descriptions, YouTube demonstrations and reviews all in one place. I experienced a "wow" over some guns that tickled my fancy. Finding what appealed to me was a great hook to keep me studying the World Wide Web. I caution you to not follow an initial purchasing impulse.

I found a website that offered airgun information and that provided technical information. Folks were often available and willing to answer questions. I read about the following before I bought: 1) Intro to airgunning; 2) Airgun definitions; 3) Advertised velocities; 4) Pellets to use; and 5) Hold sensitivity.

I would have preferred to find a gun in person. Nothing compares to holding a piece in your hands or pulling it up to your shoulder to know if it fits correctly. That was not an option and I had to settle for reading reviews. If there were frequent complaints about a feature I really cared about I considered a different gun. If you were content with an "out of the box" gun consider buying from the dealer who will let you hold or shoot it. You might save a few bucks online but if it was defective your hometown dealer will make an easier exchange. Support the people who support you! Be local, buy local.

If you think you want to buy a "tuned" gun consider buying it from a company that does tuning. You will save shipping costs and time and will not miss the gun you never saw while waiting for yours to come up in the rotation. Different dealers offered different services and you want to pick the one that is right for your budget and needs. There were dealers who would pretest a gun before shipping. Having received my first-ever two airguns in poor working condition I highly recommend tuned or pretested guns.

I did have the help of my friend Roger who had extensive airgun experience. He received and tested the guns for me and I was not stuck with two lemons with no way to return or exchange them. In summary, shopping online was helpful because it saved shopping time when I was back in the States. It was important to read the reviews and find the websites that had exactly those items for which I was looking. Most important of all, having friends to receive and inspect the shipments was a big plus.

CHAPTER 82, DAY 298, TALKING *TICO*

Day 298 and here was some more *Tico* talk... I thought I had finally put one and one together. I thought I had finally reached a deeper understanding. In the book The *Ticos*, they addressed the gossipy nature of the people. I guessed if people were going to talk about you, you might as well give them something to talk about. If not, they will make up something.

Jose was my first "guy" here in Costa Rica. He attached himself to me in hopes of future wealth under the guise of wanting to help me. I always thought it odd that when I would ask him an innocent question like, "What are you doing tomorrow?" he became extremely defensive. The cleaning lady did also. If I asked Flor how her kids were doing she would ask me why I wanted to know.

I found that odd and I replied that I was just making small talk. This was true in my case. I consistently received that type of response to innocent questions and consistently I replied I was just making small talk. They had nothing to fear from me but that did not stop them from being secretive.

Well, when I was on the other side of the questioning process I discovered the result of honest and open responses to "innocent" questions. The gal I met who worked in a *Panaderia* would call me before going to work. We would talk about general stuff and occasionally she would ask me a personal question. For example, she asked me if I were Catholic. I innocently replied "Yes I went to Catholic school as a child and was a 'believer' but did not attend church."

Little did I know that it was a loaded question? A loaded question was a qualifying question. If the qualifying question was answered incorrectly the respondent was dismissed as an unacceptable person. (Oh, the tricks we learned in sales. This was a proven method to separate likely buyers from window shoppers.)

Who would have guessed that her former husband, whom she hated, was Catholic? I was then lumped into a group of people regardless of my individual personality. So, I could see why people were reluctant to divulge information and had developed a talent of telling me what I wanted to hear. This was not just a negative perspective on my part. So it went with my *Panaderia* friend and after answering a few questions I was no longer a person of interest.

What did I know…? From my US perspective people were usually not that knee jerk, emotionally triggered and narrow minded. That was why they avoided answering questions or guessed what I wanted to hear and fed me the line they thought would make me like them. From a Costa Rican perspective they were just making me happy because they thought if they didn't that I would shun them. The *Ticos* seemed very emotionally driven. They would like me or hate me with little or no reason.

Soon enough I received my first opportunity to practice question evasion. I received a telephone call from a *Gringa*, Sharon, who was a friend of the Italian restaurant owners and I was surprised to hear her voice on the phone. She asked me if I was busy today and instead of openly and honestly answering her question (which was complicated because there was always something to do) I asked her why she wanted to know.

She then said she was going to a gathering of friends and wanted to know if I wanted to join her. Guardedness and defensiveness does not come naturally to me, but without it, nothing much else was going to come to me. I got invited once and never again… Just not their kind of person I guess? It was like walking on egg shells to have a conversation in this country. Again, I think the *Gringos* turn *Tico* rather quickly or they come here with similar temperaments.

CHAPTER 83, DAY 348, A TRIP TO THE USA.

On day 348 I had returned from editing and a trip to Oregon. I survived the trip back with screaming babies and all. Being awake for 36 hours, going to and from the US, takes a heavy toll. Next time I might try drugs to help me sleep on the plane. I was still not rested.

I had made four plumbing repairs with the hardware from Home Depot. I put away a few things. I tried out a few things and fell back into a few old routines. As much as I enjoyed my time with friends in Oregon I seemed to only miss them more when I left. It was nice to have felt loved but it only added to the realization of my lonely existence here in Costa Rica. I had occasioned the thought of separating myself from my past entirely but I felt like the lone stranger here. I cannot afford to keep flying back and forth either financially or emotionally. Though I reveled in the joy of my associations in *El Norte* I felt all the more lost and alone here after all the camaraderie up there passed.

I had to thank my long time friend, Roger, for his generous hospitality. I really appreciated the use of his house, truck, his home cooking, and his company. He helped make the trip a success by receiving and trying out products and shopping for me. It would not have been as easy without all the help and I was indebted to him.

Christine now had the Directives to Physicians and she could execute the Will, Directives, and Disposition of Remains. I thought she might use my cell phone while I was gone and I would use hers in June upon my return. Time will tell how that relationship will turn out. So far; no blood, no foul!

I checked my calendar and I needed to cross the border again between December 27 and January 12, 2011. I could go any time, for as little as one day, but I needed to go sometime during those two weeks. I might enjoy Boca Del Toro in Panama on the Caribbean coast. Boca was supposed to be real nice or San Juan Del Sur in Nicaragua had a nice beach on the Pacific Ocean... I received an invitation to meet a friend and her companions in Playa del Carmen, Mexico but I was going to Panama to check out the surf spots and housing! I might be looking to find a winter home and to renew my surfing *pasatiempo*.

I was glad I had less than 20 days of writing left and looked forward to moving off of this project. As for opening a blog site or self-publishing, I didn't feel any strong desire to move in that direction at this time. Most of my friends did not email... so, I guessed that would really create more separation. Some friends talked about visiting and we would see if that happened. Most *Gringos* tell me their friends talk about it but never show up.

Christmas was already in the stores here and prices were on the rise. It was funny how two weeks could make such a difference. When any of the Government controlled prices rose, it seemed to trigger an across the board inflationary response. When Taxi fares went up I noticed coffee shop prices rose. Electricity rates went up and I noticed that the price of cilantro had doubled.

I was not a real big shopper so it was hard to say what had risen to meet the increased costs and it did not all happen at once. In the short year I had been here I watched the cost of living continue to climb. This was still far cheaper than Northern living but it was beginning to stretch my budget. When I first arrived, my *Tipico Tico* breakfast was 1,200C and that had gone up to 1,700C, a 30% increase. With inflation at nearly 30% I would have even less money for luxuries, but enough talk about money.

CHAPTER 84, DAY 352, *TICO* FRIENDSHIP

Day 352 followed the anniversary of my mother's birth. It was sad to think that just a year ago yesterday she was dragged to an attorney's office in tears, fighting for her right to leave her bequeath to me. I did not feel bad about it. Coercion was the father of guilt and that was a horrible price for my brother to pay for a little money. OK, a large sum of money but he did not need it to live comfortably.

I still missed the camaraderie of my visit to the US. I found myself longing anew for English conversation with those I knew and loved. I'd had enough of that superficial online chatting that eventually ended with some kind of personal rejection. It was so odd that in a land where people were reportedly "so nice" there was so very little compassion and so much pent up hostility.

Here, many people smiled and/or asked "How are you?" However, it was not that they cared; it was only a social formality. In the book <u>The *Ticos*,</u> they described Costa Ricans as egocentric. Friendliness went only as far as "What did you have for me? What would you think of me? What would you say about me? And most importantly, what could I acquire from you?"

It seemed that mothers did not care about their children's feelings or well-being. The main consideration of who fathered a child seemed to be who was going to pay for his or her support and medical bills. *Que me importa* was applied to spouses and children and no one was exempt from the self interested natures that lay beneath the façade of nicety. That thinking was adopted by both *Ticos* and *Gringos* here.

Men chased women without regard for their spouses or girlfriends and women had children without concern for familial values. I grew up in a fairly dysfunctional family but I saw the value of my growing up in a family. At least my brother and I looked alike. Here, so many siblings had different parentage and were lucky if they even knew their biological fathers.

With the exception of Flor, who was still a friend, I had no contact with the women here that did not end without some kind of insult or aspersion. Closeness was shunned here and if I showed too much understanding or interest a negative rejection soon followed. *Tico* guys soon enough ignored me and/or became unavailable. At least the guys did not feel a need to be insulting.

It was like the lemonade. The *Tico* liked their sour fruits, but only with so much sugar that they could not taste the sour. They liked their strong coffee but only with enough cream and sugar that they could not taste the coffee. There were over 15 bakeries in the four square mile downtown and hardly one of them carried anything decent. As a generalization of the culture, they wanted everything but wanted to do nothing for it. It was so superficial here. It continued to serve as a constant invitation to perceive the great illusions of life that was before me.

With all the distancing and emotional abuse I suffered at the hands of my father and my brother I thought I would have taken this all in stride but it took coming here to live in a culture of emotional neglect to see that some of my friends and family were spiritually and emotionally crippled. But for the grace of God go I and then with the grace of God I went.

I suppose I chose the road to sainthood when contracting for a spot on earth. I needed to live a selfish life to find compassion for others. Like a modern day Siddhartha I needed to become a self centered and egotistical sot to feel true compassion for those living that life. There was a big enough part of me that was hard-hearted that I believed I could develop those skills with some effort.

I mentioned before that it was the giving up of insight that would be difficult. How would I grasp the concept of not understanding concepts? How did I see inside of myself enough to find the part of me that did not see inside of others? Was I smart enough to become stupefied to the feelings and motives of others? One aspect of retirement was I had plenty of time to practice.

CHAPTER 85, DAY 354, LAUNDRY

It was day 354 and long ago I promised to write a page on laundry. I wrote this from the perspective of someone without a dryer who used the old style *Tico* washer. Many homes had only a washer and clothesline. The *Tico* washer required pushing buttons to change cycles and turning the faucet on and off to fill the drum. The spin cycle was in an extra tub and I had to move the clothes from the wash to the spin tub by hand.

If I had leaned toward synthetics and silks drying would have been less of a problem. However my fine materials and even some heavy clothes had been torn up by the washer. So, I never used the heavy cycle and always had the tub full of water before starting the agitator.

Noticing that the water was so full of algae and other organic material I started to add a splash of disinfectant to the wash water because the laundry soap alone did not kill off the growth and bleach was too hard on the material. It seemed strange how even freshly laundered clothes smelled soiled almost as soon as I dressed. As the Coors Beer commercial boasts with pride: "It's the water!"

There was a product sold in Costa Rica to add to the toilet bowl that disinfects the water as it sits. Almost any pan, pot or bowl of tap water left to sit would start to smell bad. I understood why there were no p-traps under the sinks. The trap held water and began to stink quickly. There was a p-trap in my bathroom instead of straight pipe and it stunk every time fresh water agitated it. I would have been better off with straight pipe to the septic line. That would smell better.

The disinfectant had a foamy character of its own, so I needed to use very little laundry soap. I was detergent sensitive and I could not find hypoallergenic laundry soap. All the soaps and cleaners here were very strong. I washed with the delicate cycle and the water high enough to move the lint trap back and forth. After draining the tub I cycled through a few shots of fresh water while the drain cycle was on and appeared finished and then more soapy water would be expelled from the bottom of the tub. All the water levels were controlled by opening a spigot and watching the tub fill, then shutting the spigot by hand. The fill and drain cycles were also manually controlled by a switch on the machine.

When the discharge water ran clear I filled the tub for rinsing and rinsed on the gentle cycle. I drained that water with the same clearing procedure as for the wash and rinsed twice. Then everything went into the spin tub. I was careful clothes did not touch the top edge and that I did not touch the moving parts. There were plenty of sharp edges that must be intended to keep the retail clothes shops and pharmacies in business. I was sure to remove the water fill hose and drain it so algae did not grow in the hose.

Maybe even more important than how I washed clothes was when I washed clothes. If I were not an early riser it would have been a disadvantage. The best days to wash were mornings which were clear and sunny by 6 AM. I started the wash at 5 AM when I put the water on for coffee. The wash and rinse cycles took an hour and I wanted to capture the heat of the sun for drying. Gray mornings were not good wash days.

If I washed at night or late in the day my clothes stayed wet for so long they became musty and others had complained of mold growing on their clothes. Washing was one thing but drying was even more important. Synthetics would have dried more quickly but I had mostly cotton clothes and they required more attention.

First, I turned everything inside out and when they felt dry enough I turned them right side in to dry the outer part. I usually hung laundry outside in the sun. However on rainy occasions I had taken to putting a small fan in the laundry room to help with circulation of the air and I had even used the heater function when the air was really damp. Pants needed to be pinned up by the pockets and shirts were hand "ironed" while still wet. Smoothing out the wet shirts prevented wrinkles from setting in. If not dry by nightfall I brought them inside and put the fan on them overnight because there were moths here in Costa Rica. However, there was a "wash and fold" full service laundry here in Grecia for those who did not want to bother with the laundry process.

CHAPTER 86, DAY 357, PASTIMES

It was day 357 and the end of this writing project was near. I felt so perseverant! I could not believe I had been on this for almost a year. I completed the map project to the point I needed to determine which shops would not be closing. I began to doubt the value of continuing because of the shop instability and I felt there was little market for a local directory. All that work was not wasted. It had been a great excuse to walk and I really knew my way around town.

There was no market for a directory because the locals did not care about changing their routines (they shopped where they shopped and did not care about finding other places to shop). The *Gringos* knew everything and there was nothing I could tell them. Even if they didn't know they would not take advice or information, from a "new guy." With that arrogance it was easy for me to not feel any loss by being excluded from their circles.

How did US President Obama put it? I was finding comfort clinging to my guns and my religion. I brought three air guns to Costa Rica on my last trip, and they were punching single ragged holes at 45 feet. Well, I was able to hit the targets regularly ha ha ha. All the sights and scopes were dialed in and the Crosman airguns had already started to rust. I had oil and a dehumidifier to install in the gun box. I thought The Beatles put it best when they sang "Happiness is a warm gun." These guns were projects I enjoyed working on and as such they gave me hours of happy tinkering.

Now I had a *pasatiempo* that did not require social contact. As for the other 150 lbs of luggage... the plumbing was done for now. The clothes and linens were put away and I needed to study the use of the camera. A project from my April trip north still lingered and I had begun to download programs and files from the laptop to the notebook with my new flash drives. And the folks at Rosetta Stone were helpful.

The current focus of my business transactions was straightening out my banking and the earnings missing from my social security estimate. It also seemed that some people felt like I owed them something for their very existence. This was an extreme contrast from the people who had gone out of their way to help me. On that note, special thanks needed to go out to Roger and Christine again for not only lodging me on my Oregon visits but for their unending generosity.

As for clinging to religion, I focused on self love first and from that platform I believed there was plenty of love left to go around. Everybody had their good points and though I appreciated them I did not owe them for being good or even for being good to me.

I became adept at being alone and not lonely. The contrast from all the social contact I enjoyed during my US visit was huge. There just was not the same type of social fabric here in Costa Rica that existed in *El Norte*. I cannot explain it and I could not understand it even though I lived in it. I just knew I was "not in Kansas anymore."

I reminded myself that it was all about the money. After buying a house I no rent to pay and I lived on less than $400 a month. But I was not making trips in a car to $100 a night hotels and eating $25 meals. Even living as simply as possible in the US I could not have paid basic bills on $400 a month. Another consideration was that in the US there was the temptation to buy more and more and more.

I did not include my trips to the US or the money spent on those trips in my expenses. I saw those trips as temporary and the ravenous temptation to buy in the States did not exist for me here. I easily spent $1,000.00 during two weeks of casual shopping in the States. I almost ignored prices and purchased whatever called out to me. Soon enough it would all be about being Latin. Again, it was all about the finances. It was just a matter of what money I had and what money I needed to spend to live.

CHAPTER 87, DAY 360, ONLINE DATING

On day 360 I noticed how much I was a slave to convention. I never really noticed how stuck in a box I had become until I got a glimpse of the sky. I always followed the calendar and knew when spring started and fall stopped, all the phases of the seasons and declination of the sun. Nothing was the same here and when I saw that nothing was the same here I realized that nothing was as I thought it was back in *El Norte*.

Mis amigos en El Norte were just then commenting about the rain and the cold and I had seen spring-like conditions here right now. Were we all going to say that on September 21st the seasons changed? Seasons changed when they changed. The calendar had little to do with the event. Seasons varied by latitude, longitude, elevation and proximity to large bodies of water.

Here in Grecia they said the rainy season started mid-May, and that mid-March to mid-April had the most heat of summer and that mid-July to mid-August was a poor time to plant. I was not here the first two weeks of October but the swallows had returned to Grecia. That marked the beginning of spring for me, as well as the increased butterfly sightings and a profusion of flowers.

The days were warming, the rains were lightening and I was seeing more interest on the singles networking site. The farmers' market prices had just dropped that week and I was beside myself in confusion as to the giant changes in the price and the quality of the vegetables. No less confusing was the Costa Rican online dating site.

I gave up trying to make sense of the changes. Farmers' market prices and quality changed as they did and I shopped accordingly. Twenty five to thirty-year-old *Tica* beauties and fifty to sixty year old *Gringas* were all looking for the same thing and I just didn't care anymore. I take that back, the *Ticas* were looking for sex and money. However, the *Gringas* were past that stage in their lives and were just looking for the money. Gee... tough choice?

Then, I sought that delicate balance the Buddhists referred to as right effort. I was willing to slip into a state where I was exerting just the amount of effort necessary to move forward and not try to create an outcome. To that end, I bought the veggies that looked good and were not priced at out-of-season prices (out of the box of having to buy any particular produce) and I closed my profile on the singles site (out of the box of thinking there was intelligent life out there).

The price and the quality on the singles site varied wildly also. Take the last three gals to contact me on the site. One gal looked at my profile and saw my location as Grecia, Costa Rica and she asked "Where do you live?"

The next gal implied that I did not have enough money for any woman in my life because I only spent $400 a month on my living expenses. Maybe if I spent $4,000.00 a month on me there would be enough left over to support her too? I just didn't understand. I guessed it was a sin to live a simple life! I wondered how much she spent a month but I didn't care to ask.

The straw that broke the camel's back was a gal wrote and said, "Hello, How are you? I'm planning to visit Costa Rica., What travel advice do you have for me?" (Please, spare me. Were you too poor to buy a travel book but wealthy enough to visit? Did I know you? Did I owe you something because I was on a singles site?) Lucky for her I was in a generous mood and I sent her some advice. As expected, no expression of appreciation was returned upon her receipt of my sage advice.

Enough overpriced tomatoes for me. They were out-of-season, overripe and not very nourishing. I always liked those stories like Walden Pond, Siddhartha and Utopia. Were there no more followers of Henry David Thoreau, F. Buckminster Fuller and Herman Hess?

CHAPTER 88, DAY 361, TRICK OR TREAT

Day 361 Trick or Treat. Was that another paradox? As awkward as money matters were in the US, money was even more bizarre here in Costa Rica. Money, cash, dough, *dinero*, *plata* and *effectivo* are in and of themselves straight forward. I had it, I spent it, and I had what I had. There were banks and exchange rates and better interest rates paid on dollar accounts in Panama than in the US or in Costa Rica.

To secure cash you either worked, inherited, begged, stole or borrowed it. The *Ticos* tended to spend it as soon as they received it and they generally didn't even look to make money until they needed it badly. Someone once told me what my problem was (as if I had only one problem or that others hadn't a different perspective on what was wrong with me). One person told me my problem was that my life was completely blessed. (How was that for trick or treat?)

Inside the paradox of having a blessed life I have never had to "work" for anything. My life was free from effort and everything I had ever needed had just come to me. You know what I mean, like the lilies of the field kind of blessings. I admitted to that problem but had never seen the problem with it. (If you want to live like that just die and be brought back and God comes back with you.)

It appeared that there were two problems within this problem. First, I had no concept of the angst that people suffered over acquiring what they needed (or wanted and thought they needed). Another problem was that I had never had the desire to struggle and strive for the acquisition of wealth. There I missed the big boat of Judeo/Christian values. Though the teachings of Christ seemed to lean in my direction it was still not the American way. (Was Peter a bad consumer? Yes. Bad Peter!)

What that meant here in Costa Rica is that I lived life more *Tico* than *Gringo*. That meant that I again fell into a crack somewhere. The first comment a *Tico* neighbor said to me was *Usted es Rico!* (You're rich.) The house cleaner's eight-year-old daughter wanted to know what I was doing with "so many" rooms all to myself. I had been accused of attempting to solicit sex because I afforded small acts of monetary kindness and I was sure I was referred to as a *Pinche Gringo* even though I did not flaunt my wealth or possessions.

Regardless of my simple lifestyle and frugal ways I was wealthy by comparison to the typical *Tico*. This was mostly because I saved and did not squander my earnings. However, I lived in abject poverty compared to the typical *Gringo*. Most *Gringos* lived in huge homes up on the hills that made my 1000 square foot home look like a cottage. Some had cottages on their property the size of my home.

They loved their garish displays of wealth and except for their hired help they had little to do with *Tico* life. They wouldn't be found on busses or living in town or shopping where the locals shopped. Renauto from the Italian restaurant liked to carry 1,000 to 1,500 dollars in cash in his pocket at all times. Whaaaaat? Might he need to buy a car at any moment? Almost any time I saw him he had some reason to flash the cash from his pocket. It was no wonder he felt the need to keep a gun behind the counter.

My monthly electric bill was $18.00 but I had never wanted the 52 inch plasma instant on flat screen TV. Some *Gringos* pay as high as $200 a month for electricity. I used the sun to dry my clothes and I had the time and skills to do what they paid others to do. However, that lifestyle choice had me shunned from their company as they might shun a typical *Tico*.

I wrote the following to a *Gringa*: "You are the first person to ever take exception to the amount of money I spent. I did what I wanted and that was the amount of money I had to take from the bank to do it. Never had anyone ever told me that I did not spend enough money and I have had, and did have, some very wealthy friends. I didn't say they were smart, they are just rich. Maybe you know something they don't."

(Tell me, my northern friends, how bad was I? Was I ruining the global economy and the ugly American image?)

CHAPTER 89, DAY 363, ZAK ON ZEN

On day 363, I had nothing new to say. However, by popular demand, I dragged something out of the goodie box for your enjoyment. This conversation happened on "G-chat" during my ninth month in Costa Rica.

ZAK: Just remember, Oh Zen master, that letting the mind wander aimlessly is the opposite of Zen quiet mind...takes a lot of work and con-Zen-tration! Cherish the moments as we don't have forever...stay in touch...Z

PETER: Dear friend, the "whatever comes to mind" comment was supposed to be tongue in cheek. Believe me I get the drill. I even cherish the moments of distress and we may not be of the same mind...I do have forever.

ZAK: I stand corrected...it is so good that you know that...takes the pressure off present desires...

PETER: It is easy to misunderstand curt communication. I get it intellectually! I understand the drill. However...I am nothing more than human and my desires and distresses are as real as the moments of *tranquillo*. They both come and they both go. In forever I would not judge my thoughts as some better than others because they would all be good.

ZAK: Butt? By curt...only short because that's all I had time for now...not meaning to connote anything negative...to me thoughts are varied blips on the screen...I did not like them all...some may violate my values or may include a harm or negativity that I would call "bad thoughts" (to be curt) but good and bad exist as relative concepts and lord knows I've had some bad relatives...just keep thinking (thank God that what's thought and what's manifest are different!)

PETER: I laughed out loud. Thanks for the *divertido*. Curt because it was the nature of email. I too find that no matter how many words I write the message is clipped. It was something about not being in person? I can't explain it well.

Yes, we were saved! But for the grace of God go I down the path that the bad thought illuminates. To be very Zen about it even that path may be my highest aspect of being. Speaks the five-year-old still so close to the mind of God "I am doing the best I can."

We could wax on about killing in the name of God... I don't mean that. I mean the most lurid and desperate thought that might cross my mind is a gift from the divine. It is a gift for me to embrace, something to learn, something to forget, only important in that it means I think, therefore... And the relatives Oye Vey don't get me started.

ZAK: ...It seems evident that we are doing the best we can in a given moment...never the best we can imagine, only the best we can do given all current variables...oh well...when that sucks we often increase our learning curve...stopping now as we have slipped in to first person plural...time for OUR pill.

PETER: The delay got that note buried. I would say that I and maybe everyone is exercising management by crises. How does Dr. Phil put it? "How's that working for you?" Not so good? Care to try a different tact? If it aint broke don't fix it? Unfortunately, being the best I could imagine only exists in my purely spiritual plane. My body does not really want to go there. Remember the terror of bliss? Being my best was like all things; better in moderation, and don't we all know that perfect is the enemy of good?

CHAPTER 90, DAY 365, WAS IT WORTH IT?

Day 365 was the anniversary of my boarding a plane with 250 pounds of luggage to my new life. Then what? Was I any happier? Was I any smarter? Was I any more enlightened? Was my life better?

I had to answer "no" to every question, say "no" to every thought and say "no" to every person. Nancy Regan had it right with "Just say no!" To heck with "Say yes to life." Life wasn't so great before and it had definitely taken a turn for the worse albeit less costly and the weather was more pleasing.

Heck, even my flash drive picked up a virus. Yea, the AVG found a Trojan horse in the flash drive from my bringing it to a print shop to print "the book" and the house was full of ants. The bright side was that they ate their own dead and cleaned them off the floor before I was back in the office in the morning.

Of course, I would be preaching the gospel of hope and faith before long. So my angst, naked and in the Full Monty for all to see, was only temporary Even being hopeful, my life would not be better for having moved to Costa Rica. Again I would say it was cheaper but not better.

I guess it was easier to see God in myself here because it was fruitless to look outside myself in a land of strangers. Wait a minute, I was the stranger here and so it would be for all time to come. The charm I found in the noises of the neighborhood waned. I often cranked up my American radio to drown out the shrieking kids, the loud music and talk or the incessant banging of my immediate neighbor. (What were they doing over there anyway?)

It rained all day yesterday and today was still gray. That was an unusual event because most mornings were bright and sunny and were then followed by afternoon rains. I shopped on Thursdays so I hoped the rain held off. Maybe most of the *Gringos* here were testy because paradise did not bring about great improvements in their lives. Those *Gringos* said they were happy but didn't look happy.

When nerve racked I usually bit my fingernails. For whatever reason I had been brutalizing my toenails and I did not look forward to the walk to town. Louise Hay, who wrote <u>You Can Heal Your Life</u>, would say I was preoccupied with little details. Yes it was the little things that were bothering me. The big concerns were still under control. Living was cheap. I had plenty of money, it was not dangerous and the weather stayed relatively mild.

Before you even start to think about how I might be a better person by thinking differently, I want to share a story I wrote back in July before taking a "friend" off my mailing list. I wished I had saved the email but for lack of more things to do I clean my email files regularly. So, here was a rewrite:

When I was living in a lily-white hipped-out former logging town in northern California I had a Black friend named Vincent. Vincent would have been referred to as an Oreo, Black on the outside but White on the inside. He had embraced all the ethics and customs of White culture. He was intelligent, articulate, hard working, a good father to his daughter, a friend to me and we both had a large circle of friends.

He and I were in our 30's, and the 1980's seemed like a rather progressive time. One day Vincent was reporting on some awkward situation. I would not say he was complaining because he was not a complainer. Of course I wanted to help my friend and I began to tell him how he might otherwise view his predicament.

Well, he became a little unglued on me and started to tell me about his life experience in our little town. He told me about guys throwing things out of cars at him as he walked down the street, people shouting "Nigger" at him and that he was followed in stores as if he were going to steal things. I was mortified. That was not my experience or mind set and I could not comprehend that type of life. It was that moment I learned to reserve my judgment and my thinking that I knew how others should live or how they should think about life… I was not him and he was not me. We all lived different lives that are truly unfathomable to others.

EPILOGUE

Maybe somewhere in the US there is a temperate climate that does not generate tremendous heating or air conditioning bills. In Oregon I was able to burn wood for heat to augment my electric heaters but I think the cost of the firewood began to rival the electric costs. Anyway, I was toasty warm in my 1,600 square foot home with the fire going and snow on the roof.

I supported vehicles because there was not a good transit system where I lived and using a taxi was outrageously expensive. Blessed with my relative youth and good health I was able to walk most places but not everywhere. However, the roads were in great repair and the sidewalks as well. By global standards the cost of petrol was inexpensive and insurance was reasonable enough.

Then there was the house payment… I'm sure you see the picture. With all the above expenses I did not mention buying food. Food prices seemed to be rising as work and income were declining. I made pretty good money when working (what was I going to do when I could not work any longer?).

On one chilly day in November of 2008 I was chopping wood, as I had for the previous 17 years, and I said to myself, "Forget this!"(Well, actually, it was another word that began with an 'F.') "I want to live somewhere warm." The money concern was not in the front of my mind at that moment but the move was something I had been contemplating for some time.

Two years before the date of this writing I was looking at an atlas for a temperate place on the planet to hang my hat. I had considered many different places, and the good money was on Costa Rica. Five months later I was on an exploratory trip to Costa Rica. It was a country into which I could afford to immigrate. Eight months after that I had shed my American coil and was living full time in Costa Rica.

Now I find myself a financial refugee living a life I can afford. I wrote this account of my experiences when I was moved to do so. This book was extracted from a one year account that began during the Northern Holiday Season and ended in the Costa Rican Springtime. It all began with what I thought I knew about Costa Rica and selling all my possessions and transplanting myself into <u>Costa Rica Retirement: Living on $400 per month</u>. What had unfolded was the discovery of the value of faith in myself and in the divine mystery that unfurls before us all like a flag to be followed through life.

I am committed to traveling the path on this treasure map and there is no returning to life in those United States. However, there may be no reaching the destination either. If I had paid too much attention to the details of what Costa Rica was like I might not have started this journey. I would have then been the poorer for not exploring the life as a "blue eye" in a land of brown eyed people.

May you not experience my trials and tribulations. After reading of my experiences you will certainly not have to make the same mistakes I made. You can make your own new mistakes and gain from what you learn.

CPSIA information can be obtained
at www.ICGtesting.com
Printed in the USA
LVHW082135290123
738190LV00024B/605

9 781502 586766